Just Therapy

- a journey

a collection of papers from the Just Therapy Team New Zealand

by

Charles Waldegrave, Kiwi Tamasese,
Flora Tuhaka & Warihi Campbell

Dulwich Centre Publications
ADELAIDE, SOUTH AUSTRALIA

ISBN 0 9577929 8 0

Copyright © 2003 by
Dulwich Centre Publications
Hutt St PO Box 7192
Adelaide 5000, South Australia
phone (61-8) 8223 3966, fax (61-8) 8232 4441
email: dcp@senet.com.au
website: www.dulwichcentre.com.au

Chapter 2 was originally published in G. Burford & J. Hudson (eds) 2000: *Family Group Conferencing: New directions in community centred child and family practice.* New York: Aldine de Gruyter. Republished here with permission. Copyright remains with Aldine de Gruyter.

Chapter 3 was originally published in the *Journal of Feminist Family Therapy*, 5(2), 1993. Republished here with permission.

Chapter 7 was originally published in M. McGoldrick (ed) 1998: *Re-visioning Family Therapy: Race, culture and gender in clinical practice.* New York: Guilford Press. Republished here with permission. Copyright remains with Guilford Press.

Printed and manufactured by
Graphic Print Group, Richmond, South Australia.

Contents

Spirituality

Maori ways

Samoan ways

Matters of gender

Working on issues of violence and abuse

Preface

Dear Reader,

I would like to extend a warm welcome to you as you delve into this significant collection of papers from The Just Therapy Team, of Wellington, New Zealand. These writings offer an account of the work of Maori, Samoan and Pakeha (European) members of the Just Therapy Team whose work has, over the last two decades, paved the way for a re-examination of the theoretical underpinnings informing family therapy and community work. What's more, their work and writings have significantly contributed to the development of practices with which to respond to social inequities of poverty, racism, sexism and structural unemployment.

The Just Therapy Team is internationally known for its passionate engagement and willingness to address serious issues. The papers in this book question the assumptions of western social science and highlight the need for those of us who are part of white western culture to step outside of taken-for-granted practices and develop ways of working which privilege matters of culture and gender. They invite us to take seriously and treat with great respect the stories of history, ancestral genealogy, gender, culture and socioeconomic status of those with whom we work, and to take steps towards building meaningful cultural and gender partnerships.

Significantly, the Just Therapy Team has played, and continues to play, a pivotal role in enabling many Australian colleagues to face the history of this country and to acknowledge the ongoing effects of colonisation on the lives of Indigenous Australians. The hand of friendship offered by the Just Therapy Team and their longstanding willingness to stand beside colleagues, workers and organisations from different parts of the world who are working to address the effects of colonisation, trauma and structural inequities, has meant a great deal to many of us. We thank them most sincerely for this.

Finally, this book is a celebration. While there is still much work to be done, the last two decades have seen significant changes in how the field of family therapy and narrative practice respond to matters of culture, gender and poverty. The influence of the Just Therapy Team in these developments has been considerable. The writings included here reflect the determination, vigour and commitments of Charles Waldegrave, Kiwi Tamasese, Flora Tuhaka and Warihi Campbell and those with whom they are closely linked. I have no doubt that you will recognise this as you read their words.

Shona Russell
on behalf of Dulwich Centre Publications

Just Therapy

1.

Just Therapy

by

Charles Waldegrave

Therapy can be a vehicle for addressing some of the injustices that occur in a society. It could be argued that in choosing not to address these issues in therapy, therapists may be inadvertently replicating, maintaining, and even furthering, existing injustices. A 'Just Therapy' is one that takes into account the gender, cultural, social and economic context of the persons seeking help. It is our view that therapists have a responsibility to find appropriate ways of addressing these issues, and developing approaches that are centrally concerned with the often forgotten issues of fairness and equity. Such therapy reflects themes of liberation that lead to self-determining outcomes of resolution and hope.

Introduction: The New Zealand and agency context

In all our therapeutic work we have endeavoured to relate to, and incorporate, the current issues that make up the New Zealand social and economic context. These include: the struggles to address the injustices to the indigenous Maori of New Zealand, and initiate an equitable partnership based on the Treaty of Waitangi (see page 59); the emerging consciousness and implications of New Zealand colonisation and consequent responsibilities to Pacific people; the marginalisation and increasing poverty of people and families on low incomes, as a result of deregulated economic and labour markets; and the attempts to address the inequities that persist between men and women as the rigidities of patriarchal webs of meaning are loosened.

Our agency structure has developed over the years to reflect our response to these issues. There are Maori, Samoan, and European (white) therapists who work, each from their own self-determining sections. The workers in these sections carry out family therapy and community development work in the fields of poverty, unemployment, housing, sexism, and racism.

This approach emerged ten years ago after we realised, during one of our six monthly reflective retreats, that many families were approaching our agency for therapy with problems which were not intrinsic to the family, but imposed by broader social structures. These included: families where members were unemployed; those living in inadequate housing conditions; the victim survivors of abuse; or cultures that were marginalised by the dominant culture.

Our retreats involve five days together in a large house beside a beautiful lake. We analyse and reflect on our work over the past six months, and set our goals for the following six months. At this particular retreat, about ten years ago, we realised that the problems these families were bringing to us were not the symptoms of family dysfunction, but the symptoms of broader structural issues like poverty, patriarchy, and racism. We, like most other therapists, were treating their symptomatic behaviour as though it were a family problem, and then sending them back into the structures that created their problems in the first place. We recognised that we were unwittingly adjusting people to poverty or the other forms of injustice by addressing their symptoms, without affecting the broader social and structural causes.

This realisation led us to set aside resources and initiate a community development base to our work. Over time we slowly and sensitively became involved with Maori and Pacific Island communities in our area. We then employed members of these communities in our agency who focussed on the issues facing their own people, adopting welfare thought to social policy initiatives. They also worked with the family therapists, and developed culturally appropriate ways of bringing the resources of therapy to their own people.

The co-operative work between the cultural sections has led to a number of interesting organisational processes. For example, all the workers in the agency, including those who type and receive people, take home the same salary. All work that involves someone from the Maori or Pacific Island communities is accountable directly to that cultural section. Likewise, gender work including that carried out in men's groups is directly accountable to the women in the agency. This is to ensure that a therapy is judged as just, primarily by the group that has been treated unjustly. Various ways of doing things that are uncommon to European culture, but central to Maori or Pacific Island cultures, are adopted. For example, we eat communally, make decisions consensually, receive and farewell guests formally and traditionally, and we share and express different forms of spirituality.

We are a small agency with eleven staff. Each cultural section has male and female workers so that we can appropriately address cultural and gender issues in ways that do justice to both. Because staff work in both the community development and family therapy fields, experiences from one inform the other. A family therapist may, for example, work on emergency housing, community organising, and housing policy projects in their community development work. This experience broadens their understanding and responses to people coming for therapy who are inadequately housed. Likewise, the feelings of self-blame and helplessness often expressed by unemployed people when a community worker is involved in a project with unemployed people, are able to be addressed by a worker who is experienced and knowledgeable in therapeutic work.

As a group, a number of underlying assumptions to our work have emerged over the years. They are reflected in all the work that we do and are, therefore, worthy of note in this introduction. They can be summarised under three headings:

Spirituality, Justice and Simplicity

Since spirituality informs every aspect of life in Maori and Pacific Island cultures, it naturally plays an important role in a great deal of our work. Instead of the traditional European dualistic world view that separates physical and spiritual values, we have learned to respect the sacredness of all life. Spirituality for us is not centred on organised religion, but on the essential quality of relationships, and refers to the relationship between people and their environment, people and other people, people and their heritage, and people and the numinous.

We view the process of therapy as sacred. People come, often in a very vulnerable state, and share some of their deepest and most painful experiences. For us, these stories are gifts that are worthy of honour. The therapists honour them by listening respectfully for their meaning, and offering new meanings which enable resolution, hope and self-determination. This process necessitates a high view of humanity and relationships, and as such is sacred.

Justice highlights equity in relationships between people: it involves naming the structures, and the actions that oppress and destroy equality in relationships. This is reflected in families at the micro level, and beyond that to the social structures at the macro level. Just therapy must always take both into account. Unfortunately, the resources of therapy have been largely utilised by one group of people. In most Western societies, it is the middle-class groups, and they get most of the other resources as well. A just therapy ensures that those most in need, like those on low incomes and those cultures that are oppressed, receive the resources of therapy in a manner that addresses their daily experiences of inequity.

Effective therapy, in our view, should reflect simplicity! It does not of necessity involve complex knowledges or processes, otherwise most societies before the advent of modern science would not have been able to resolve their families' problems. In essence, the therapy we offer finds its expression in the movement in meaning from problem-centred patterns, to new possibilities of resolution and hope. Therapists listen for the meanings as people articulate their problems and the way they understand them. Therapists then offer alternative and liberating meanings of those same events.

It is this essentially simple exchange that determines the nature and gives quality to the therapy. It follows from this that people from particular cultures have expertise in the meanings associated with their culture, just as women have particular expertise to understand women's stories. This expert knowledge is at least as important as expertise in the body of Western psychological knowledge.

What is Just Therapy?

'Just Therapy' is a reflective approach to therapy developed with colleagues over eleven years at The Family Centre in New Zealand. It is termed 'Just' for a number of reasons: firstly it indicates a 'just' approach within the therapy to the client group, one which takes into account their gender as well as the cultural, social, and economic context. Secondly, the approach attempts to demystify therapy (and therapists) so that it can be practised by a wider range of people including those with skills and community experience or cultural knowledge. These people may lack an academic background, but nevertheless have an essential ability to effect significant change. It is just (or simply) therapy, devoid of the commonly accepted excesses and limitations of some professional approaches and Western cultural bias.

The term 'Just Therapy' could suggest a dilution of therapeutic knowledge and competence, and could imply a general counselling framework for non-specialised therapeutic work – a sort of social therapy that may improve our ability to address racism and poverty, rather than psychotic illnesses and the more serious psychosomatics, for example. We believe that this 'professional' reflex, not uncommon in clinical circles, may have helped create mythical boundaries around therapy, which have restricted its practice, clientele and effectiveness.

Far from being a dilution, 'Just Therapy' attempts a distillation of therapeutic practices. Though it encourages novel and more effective ways of working with poor families for example, its techniques also offer improved approaches to working with those who are socio-economically comfortable. Likewise the significance given to cultural processes and patterns of communication not only enables therapy to be more accessible and effective with Black, Hispanic, or Polynesian groups, for example, but also highlights, by contrast, the significance of socio-cultural experience in therapy for white middle-class groups.

'Just Therapy' attempts to extract the essence of therapy, which relates to the manner in which people give meaning to experience and create their 'reality'. Both therapists and clients weave webs of meaning (Bateson 1972, 1980; Maturana & Varela 1980, 1987; White & Epston 1989; Waldegrave 1989) around the problems presented in therapy. This therapy, in essence, concerns the movement from problem-centred stories of pain, to stories of resolution and hope; new meaning is given to experience, by the skilful weaving of new patterns.

This therapy is equally valuable for people who have psychotic problems, for example, as it is for those people broken as a result of being unemployed. In both examples the meaning ascribed to the problem has to be addressed, and new meanings that encourage creative change responses developed. However, the focus for the psychotic case will probably be more on intra-psychic and family communication than for the unemployed case. While these emphases would certainly have their place with the unemployed, the social, community, and political meanings would also be very significant: high levels of unemployment trace their origins to economic and political policies rather than individual motivation.

Thus 'Just Therapy' rejects the commonly accepted boundaries around therapy whereby practice is limited to intra-psychic, individual, couple, family or group work. As we have noted, broader contextual approaches to therapy are absolutely essential. Take, for example, a seriously depressed adult whose work and general expectations of happiness have been truncated as a result of restructuring and subsequent redundancy in the workplace. The significance given to work in the society, and the implications of increasing free market policies in Western economies are as important to healing as the intra-psychic work. This does not suggest that one is more important than the other. 'Just Therapy' simply complements modern approaches to therapy with information and method that is usually considered outside the parameters of clinical practice. These include social, gender, cultural, and political data as it is appropriate. Thus any work with a family where the problem centres around a father's violent abuse will, of necessity, include qualitative information on the nature and development of patriarchy. The abuse will be addressed in relation to its immediate effects on family members, but also its association with the control men exercise over so many aspects of society and the violence implicated within sexist structures.

'Just Therapy' is essentially concerned with the often forgotten issues of justice in therapy, but it also attempts to effect the change in people's lives which characterises therapy. These two aspects complement each other. In our view, broader social and political change, like therapeutic change, is essentially about giving new meaning to the world of experience.

Weaving threads of meaning

In essence then, therapy is concerned with the manner in which people give meaning to experience and, in so doing, define 'their realities'. People seek therapy when 'their problem' has become so central to their perceptions and experience that they tend to interpret other experience in the light of it, either directly or indirectly.

People who have been sexually abused during childhood, for example, often consider themselves less worthy, less competent, or less valuable than other people. This belief in their unworthiness frequently develops into a meaning system revolving around failure. As a result, often experiences which others receive as marks of competence and success, they may view as confirmations of their failure. They may define a stable relationship with periods of conflict that are usually resolved, for example, as being unhappy, too dependent, unloving, or in some way inadequate. Although their partner and close friends experience it as authentic and loving, their belief system filters out meanings associated with their competence, pleasure, and capacity to be loved. Furthermore, they may attain a high level of recognition at work or in some creative artistic arena, but pass this off as the result of someone else's action, unsatisfying, or of low value. Over time, this continuous assigning of information about their experience to categories of failure or inadequacy can become seriously depressing and self destructive.

When such a story emerges which dominates the experience of the person and their family, leading them in turn to therapy, then essentially the task of the therapist, in our view, is to facilitate new meanings which encourage the development of new stories of resolution and hope. We believe that to facilitate new meaning, 'political' as well as 'clinical' responses are required. Using the example of abuse again, in political terms (in the sense of decision-making power and judgement), sexual abuse perpetrated on a child is a brutal act, regardless of whether or not the child had other good experiences with that person. Politically speaking, the child is innocent of fault. S/he is a surviving victim of imposed actions.

Clinical work that addresses suicidal feelings, periods of depression, or unhappy sexual experience, but does not address the underlying political agendas, will merely be incorporated into the old meaning filter. This raises important ethical issues. Such symptoms may be contained for a while but new information eventually penetrates and acts upon the old filter. It is the political (ethical) work in association with the clinical work (in the narrow sense of the term) that will transform the meaning system which we have called the filter. The new meaning enables new stories of resolution and hope. The block to feelings of self-worth and confidence is transformed to attract them.

When describing therapy, we use the analogy of weaving. Although the symbolism of weaving is international, it is particularly appropriate in this context because it evokes the activity of many women in the South Pacific Ocean. People come with problem-centred patterns, and the therapist's task is to weave new threads of meaning and possibility that give new colour and new textures. For example, we consider the inability of many psychiatric hospitals and much clinical work to heal patients relates to the patterns of meaning they ascribe to the problem which serve to perpetuate the problem. A web of meaning that defines people as 'sick patients' with 'such and such' a psychiatric illness denies the presence of competence and self-determination. This is further compounded by the institutionalising practices that occur in many psychiatric hospitals or units. This type of structure can perpetuate a malignant meaning pattern, while it combats symptoms with drug therapy and narrow symptom-focussed clinical work.

The point we are making is that the sickness/patient analogy is also a pattern, full of meaning. It is as much a political statement as it is a clinical one. Ironically, it ascribes a particular status, ability, and set of expectations. Furthermore, it is a creation of the therapist. Another therapist may describe the same experiences that person or family has as 'loving' or 'competent' or 'normal under the circumstances'; this therapist weaves a very different pattern with other colours and textures which lead to different status, ability, and expectations.

For example, we worked with a family where the father and husband had spent the best part of a year in two psychiatric hospitals. He had been severely depressed and manifested psychotic symptoms. He would spend large periods of the day staring ahead and saying nothing. Instead of joining with the various mental health professionals who searched for causes, created sickness labels, used drug therapy, and tried to persuade him to participate with his family again, we:

> ... *congratulated him on how loving and caring we thought he was. 'We don't meet many people who do the things you do, Rick.' When he couldn't protect, care, or breadwin for his family, his loving response was to do everything to find out the cause of his depression, and to get it out of himself. We said we saw him as a person who wanted to get to a hospital and find out how to get this problem 'fixed up'. He was not prepared to accept second best. He'd been willing 'to give up his home, give up his work, give up everything' to get this 'fixed up'. We thought this was a sign of someone who really cared for his family.*

This approach offered a totally new meaning to his experience. The diagnosis sent to us from the psychiatrist referred to his state as: major depressive episode (severe with catatonic features); alcohol abuse; premorbid schizoid and obsessional personality traits.

He considered he was seriously sick to the point of being crazy and in need of ongoing psychiatric care. He also believed he had failed his family. The new meaning offered suggested that he had taken two deliberate and responsible decisions. Firstly, he had sacrificed his home, work, and everything that was familiar to him; and, secondly, he had done so in order to be admitted to hospital where he would receive the treatment necessary to restore his health.

Alongside the pathological meaning he ascribed to his sickness, we offered in a tone similar to his mechanical speech, this more responsible self-determining perspective. He was a bulldozer driver who spoke of depression having 'got into him' and his needing to get 'fixed up'.

Subsequently we spoke with Sharon, his wife, explaining that we noted:

... that she had sacrificed his contribution to the home and had 'stood with him through all of this'. We said that although she gives her love to him she realises it's not enough to get this depression out of him. She feels defeated by this. So she releases him and, in fact, 'discharges him to the hospital where they can nurture and look after him'. This gives her a break, so she can give him her best when he comes home next time. Like him, she doesn't want second best in this relationship either.

As with the approach to Rick, this totally new meaning impacted on the old system. She believed she had failed him because she could not keep him well; she also believed she had a crazy and irresponsible husband. Our new meaning suggested that she had assessed the situation and had committed herself to sacrifice his roles in the family and arranged for him to go to hospital and get help. She loved him and had been very responsible. Furthermore, she gives her best to him when he comes home. Playing on the word 'discharge', we recognised her status in a medical sense. Again, we offered a responsible and self-determining perspective to the events she described.

Finally, we thanked the children for their memory and help. We also assured them that nothing they had done had caused their father's sickness.

The message at the end of the second interview was paradoxical, illustrating another way in which meaning can be changed. Rick had degenerated over the year in hospital, despite psychotherapy, anti-depressant, and anti-psychotic drug therapy, and even electro-convulsive therapy. We decided to affirm their story and 'prescribe more of it' since all previous work to oppose the symptoms had failed:

We said we thought Rick had a very serious depression, and we noticed that this sort of depression sometimes happened to people who lived in rural areas where hard work was highly regarded. Rick had worked very hard. In fact, he was an equal to his wife in work who had also worked very hard. (Rick worked all week for a company and ran his own business all weekend. Sharon was still doing housework most evenings after 1 am.) He had been a good provider, protector, husband, and father. We had realised that he had worked harder than us because we had at least taken time off during some weekends over the years. He now had decided to take a rest. He stopped work and has been catching up on the rest which normal people have had throughout their life. To ensure he was rested properly, he got really depressed so no-one would get him back to work. This type of depression really requires a long rest.

We went on to say that Sharon really understands this; after all she is his partner. She had said that 'half of her was missing' with him in hospital. We were impressed with the way she had taken over many functions from him. She received phone calls 8-11 times a day from him asking her advice on what he should do next. She got everything for him when he was home, and even decided when he should cuddle her. 'She works for him, thinks for him, and feels for him.' We thought it was very helpful that she had taken over all these things because that enabled him to get some proper rest.

He could concentrate on staring and 'you can't get more rest than that'. We noted that the children were getting their mother to do all sorts of things for them that other kids their age would do themselves. In this way they were like their father.

Finally we said we thought everyone was being very sensible, but that they could try a bit harder. We encouraged Rick to stare more and to telephone for advice whenever he was about to change activities. We also suggested Sharon have more contact with Rick so she could direct him more. By taking over more she could help him rest through staring. Finally we suggested it was not advisable to get better quickly, and we cautioned them against any activity that would get in the way of Rick's rest.

Between the third and fourth interviews, Sharon concluded that carrying everything for Rick and the family was absurd. She decided to leave her children with her sister while she took the unusual step of going on holiday. She rang Rick and told him. He was disturbed by the change in Sharon and decided that he desperately needed to get out of hospital to look after the children. Unfortunately for him, there was a committal order on his stay in hospital so he had to prove to the medical staff that he was well enough to leave. Rick's staring stopped, he became very concerned with his family responsibilities and eventually was discharged after 10 days. Within two weeks he had found a local bulldozing job and a month later the family was reporting life as 'back to normal again'. Rick was even joking with me in the fifth interview.

We consider that it was the sickness definition that restricted Rick's progress. That definition assigned him a dismal status and expectations and destroyed his motivation and hope. It also affected Sharon, suggesting to her that she needed to be a totally self-sufficient adult in the house, thus leaving no room for the unconfident Rick. When he believed he was needed, that there was a gap that he should fill in the family, his beliefs and expectations of himself changed dramatically. This enabled a change in his motivation; he took hold of himself and became self-determining once again.

This is not to suggest that we should never categorise people's problems and close all our psychiatric institutions. Furthermore, this is not a 'cheap shot' at psychiatry or drug therapy, all of which have their place and even successes. Rather, it is intended to emphasise that central to practically all therapeutic problems is meaning, whose created pattern determines the manner in which the problem is responded to.

As a therapist engages with a person, or family, they soon offer their strands of interpretation, bringing different colours and textures to the meaning. It is the interaction of these strands with the existing meaning patterns that, we contend, determines successful or unsuccessful therapy. Every time therapists respond during interviews, and particularly when they speak, they are adding to the meaning pattern of their client, and this is the essence of therapy. We consider it the essence because it has the potential to change the person's, or family's, meaning web, and thus the way they view the problem.

Therefore, when therapists use a physical science model to seek the 'correct diagnosis' with the 'right interpretation or explanation' in order to 'treat' the 'pathology', they frequently further entrench the problem-centred web of meaning by further defining it. Those seeking help incorporate these threads of advice and definition into their problem-centred web. Thus the meaning created in therapy can actually strengthen their problem's influence over them, offering scientific explanations for its onset and persistent domination.

As we said before, problem-centred webs of meaning persist by acting as the filter through which people interpret their experience. The meaning given to those experiences reflects the pattern created around the problem. This web of meaning remains quite intact by many (though not all) traditional therapeutic techniques including: sickness labels; symptom-focussed work; listening that simply understands the problem; and simple information concerning possible causes and explanations of the problem.

Furthermore, therapeutic work that does not reflect the underlying and surrounding socio-cultural threads of meaning will, in all probability, be rejected or incorporated in such an ill-fitting manner that the pattern will be full of tension. People's culture, their living conditions, and their gender, are crucial determinants of the meaning patterns they create.

The teaching of therapy in practically all academic institutions, however, has been mono-cultural. Concepts deeply imbedded in modern North American and Western European societies have been presented as the international and intercultural ways of therapy. Further, the social context of those most in need of health and welfare resources, such as housing, employment and an adequate income, seldom affects the therapeutic task. It is neatly confined to some other worker or institution, leaving the therapist free to get on with the 'real' therapeutic task. It is the culture of the particular person, however, which probably determines more than any other factor, the underlying structure of their meaning system. Inevitably, people's ability to access resources like food and housing significantly influences their construction of reality. It is little wonder that therapeutic work with the poor, and those from non-Western cultures has been so ineffective.

Feminist therapists and writers, on the other hand, have not been slow to point to the politics inherent in therapy. They have raised the issues of power in families and the preservation, through therapy, of patriarchal patterns of inequity. By addressing the gender context of women politically, they have revealed that much therapy has created ill-health among women because the underlying patriarchal-meaning web was not addressed. The cure of family symptoms has often been approached in a clinical vacuum, bereft of significance and meaning. Inevitably new symptoms appear, because the same meaning web continues to interpret the experience.

When describing therapy we have previously said:
Instead of addressing a known pathology, therapists engage in conversation, listening respectfully for the articulation of meaning by the person or family. The conversation enables the generation of new meaning by the therapist. The threads that the family have woven into a problem-focussed pattern are joined by new threads of new colour with different meanings that encourage new possibilities, or ways of resolution and hope. (Waldegrave 1989)

Culture

The preoccupation in clinical circles with scientific and medical meaning systems has sent therapists scurrying after 'the real causes', 'the real explanations' and 'the real cures', as though they were addressing events in the physical world, like earthquakes or the spread of AIDS. These meaning systems have required them to be rigorously 'scientific', 'neutral', and 'professional'. It was as though people's therapeutic problems were entities in themselves, and the humanity and meaning from which those problems spring are disregarded. This is not to suggest the therapists and researchers were necessarily inhumane or cold, but that the meaning system that underpins their therapeutic pursuit was understood best as physical, scientific, biological, and medical analogies.

This search for objective diagnoses, causes, explanations, and cures, has separated therapeutic problems from the social and cultural contexts out of which they develop. It is little wonder therefore that our psychiatric and psychological knowledge is, in fact, very restricted and tentative. It has been the analogies of 'construction', 'story', and 'weaving' that have removed the restrictions of physical scientific investigation from therapeutic discussion and relocated it within this arena of meaning.

The 'constructivist approach' (Maturana & Varela 1980, 1987) to therapy requires the search and pursuit of meaning. Furthermore, it requires therapists to become acutely aware of the meaning construction they create in therapy. This awareness must inevitably lead to the cultural determinants of people's meaning webs.

Cultures carry within them history, beliefs, ways of doing things, and processes of communication. Experience of the most intimate events and the most public are interpreted to people, to some considerable extent, by their culture: culture, by its very nature, gives meaning to events and experience. This, in our view, requires of the therapist a qualitative appreciation and informed knowledge of a particular culture if therapy is to be successful in an ongoing sense. A family's story, their woven pattern, is significantly shaped by their culture, and the new threads of meaning have to sit comfortably with that culture.

This may seem obvious, but very little attention has been paid to it in therapeutic conferences, writing and teachings. With the exception of a few creative attempts, such as those of family therapists, Boyd-Franklin (1989), and McGoldrick, Pearce & Giordano (1982), 'tourist therapy', the term we coined in 1985 (Waldegrave 1986), is unfortunately much more common:

> *There now exists a method of working that has become all too common, which I wish to term 'tourist therapy'. This is therapy that operates with about as much cultural understanding and sensitivity as your average package tourist en route. It moves, as if from hotel to jetplane, and flies over all that is indigenous. Brief and unconvincing attempts are made by the therapist to appreciate the client family's perspective, during a long process of cross-cultural collisions, most of which the therapist is totally unaware of. These serve to close rather than open the family's involvement and confidence in therapy. At the same time they add weight to the therapist's growing list of evidence of the family's dysfunction. Stereotypic conclusions are often reached, and eventually the therapist retires without initiating any real change in the family system. S/he then returns to the more predictable Anglo-Saxon systems somewhat bemused, like a tourist arriving home having seen the world but having learnt little about it.*

As we have already noted, successful approaches in therapy are often presented as being somehow international and intercultural. Psychological knowledge is, by implication, considered simply sufficient in itself to address the problems of people, regardless of culture and background. Our work in a New Zealand agency, with staff and clients from three cultures – Maori, Samoan, and European (white) – strongly suggests this is a false conclusion.

Concepts of self and individual assertiveness, for example, are products of individualistic Western living. They owe much to the 'Protestant ethic' and the need of modern economic systems to isolate and entrap as many individual consumer units as possible. Destiny, responsibility, legitimacy, and even human rights, are viewed by Western European and North American people as being essentially individualistic qualities.

Because so much modern social science has been developed within these cultures, individual self-worth is usually seen as a primary goal of therapy. However, people from communal and extended family cultures do not relate easily to concepts of 'self'. For them, questioning that refers directly to self-exposure, or self-assertion, is often very confusing. To make sense of such questioning, the person has to reflect on a total family consensus.

Questioning relating to self alienates people because it crudely crashes through the developed sensitivities prevalent in communal-based cultures, where identity is expressed in extended family, rather than individual terms. The questioning is experienced by these people as intrusive and rude. Furthermore, such questioning ruptures the co-operative sensitivity among people in such cultures, sensitivity which provides the framework of essential meaning required for resolution of their problems.

Maori and Samoan people in New Zealand, for example, usually prefer to address problems they may have together with their families, rather than on an individual basis. Sometimes one person will be accorded spokesperson's rights for the family on a particularly sensitive issue, like sexual abuse for example. That person's pattern of meaning comes from the family as a whole and requires the same sort of attention as the many individual voices in a European family. Attempts to draw other family members into the discussion will be met with embarrassment and resistance. Other members of the family can be addressed when that story has been fully told.

When other members are addressed, however, there are cultural sensitivities that require attention. It is not acceptable for a young person to disagree openly with his/her parents. A question that invites an evaluative judgement of an adult relative's analysis of events will simply lead to silence and the lowering of eyes on the part of the young person. If a therapist wants to find out that person's opinions on a particular matter that has already been discussed, the question needs to be asked later in the interview in such a way that it won't involve disagreement with, or evaluation of, the older person's statement. Communication in these cultures is very sophisticated and often requires subtlety and indirect processes that are less common and more complex than in most European and North American cultures.

Therapists in Western countries have deluded themselves for long enough by dismissing this sort of information as irrelevant in their society. A closer look at most Western societies, however, reveals that there are numbers of indigenous, non-white, and/or communally-based cultures in all our countries and most of our cities. Furthermore, social deprivation statistics usually feature people from these cultures in disproportionately large numbers in areas such as unemployment, poor housing, low educational attainment, poor health, high crime rates, and so on. In other words, these people are more in need of the health and welfare resources of our countries than most other groups.

The sad conclusion we have reached is that therapists, generally speaking, have added to the problems these people experience by imposing Western meaning structures on them regardless of their own culture's meaning webs. The education systems, economic systems, the media systems, and all the other structures that create meaning in society have forced an alien meaning structure onto them. It is this primary difference, when cultural experience is far removed from, and often contradicts, the systems of control in a society, that is usually identified as the prime cause of 'failure to achieve'.

Therapy that does not address cultural meaning webs in informal ways simply continues the process of alienation. A symptom may be resolved but, in the process, people's primary meaning webs are devalued and they are subsequently distanced from their closest relations. Although it may be unintentional, such therapy should be seen as 'racist'.

This is because racism is not simply about individual prejudice and bigotry. Most cultures have their share of that. Racism exists when that prejudice is exercised by the culture whose values and beliefs dominate the institutions and structures of a given society. In other words, when the prejudice is coming from the group whose cultural experience and the systems of control in society are essentially in harmony. This is usually referred to as institutional racism. It directly affects Blacks, Indians, and Hispanics in the United States, for example, just as it affects Maori and Pacific Island people in New Zealand, or the Aboriginal people of Australia.

Many white people say they are not racist because they do not think black people are inferior, and they believe they should have an equal chance of 'success' along with everyone else. According to this view, everybody in Western democracies has essentially the same opportunities: therefore their society is not racist. This argument is both very common and very ill-informed. It is preoccupied with individual intentions and beliefs, and totally ignores the social and institutional realities.

> *The disregard that many therapists have of the integral part spirituality plays in the life of people from non-Western cultures offers another example of this process. Nancy Boyd-Franklin (1989) states: Training in the mental health fields largely ignores the role of spirituality and religious beliefs in the development of the psyche and its impact on family life. In the treatment of Black families, this oversight is a serious one.*

In our experience, dreams, feelings, prayers, and 'other-worldly' experiences are an essential aspect of therapeutic conversation experienced with most Maori and Samoan families. This is often disregarded, considered irrelevant, or, worse still, treated as evidence of naivety and ignorance by therapists. In an attempt to be 'scientific', such activity is often viewed suspiciously and neatly side-stepped to make way for the 'real stuff'. In our work with Maori people we have found it quite impossible to carry out successful therapy without acknowledging the *wairua* (spiritual) side. It is not uncommon for the realisation of the significance of a dream to change the whole family system. This is because spirituality in many cultures is an integral and essential part of their meaning patterns.

There are many other ways cultures determine meaning for people and should be taken into account when they present for therapy. We have noted, for example, significant differences between cultures as a result of their history, for example, immigration or war trauma; their language and the manner in which it promotes certain concepts but reduces others; their definitions of acceptable and unacceptable behaviour; the associated concepts of respect and shame; patterns of thinking and communication – circular or linear patterns; family structures – boundaries and decision-making; and the degree of affirmation or subjugation of their culture; and ways of doing things in the society they live in.

All of these influence the meaning people attribute to events and experience. And it is out of these meanings that problems emerge and resolutions and healing can be affected. Good therapy engages authentically with people's woven pattern of meaning, and then in appropriate ways weaves new threads of resolution and hope that blend with, but nevertheless change, the problem-centred design.

As we have stated, culture is probably the most influential determinant of meaning in people's lives. Cultures express the development of humanity and co-operation of groups of people over long periods of time. As such they are sacred and worthy of the greatest respect.

Cultures are not learned or understood by scientific observation, but experienced by living. People who are from a particular culture can articulate the processes and finer nuances of that culture. As a way of respecting the two Polynesian cultures we have worked with in New Zealand, we have not controlled the therapeutic work with people from those communities. This is a very important principle, because of the domination of European values and social structures in New Zealand society.

We had been working as a family therapy agency for a number of years in New Zealand, when it became obvious to us that Maori and Pacific Island people had no real access to the resources and skills of family therapy. This was because the therapists were part of the white community and had been practising with people of their own background. Maori and Pacific Island people are discriminated against in New Zealand and therefore have the highest rates of unemployment, highest sickness rates, lower educational achievement, and so on. It became important for us to address this problem.

Our organisation decided to take time to develop close links with the Maori and Pacific Island communities. We also set aside resources to provide employment for workers from those communities. Then over a period of time we shared with them the sorts of things we were doing in family therapy. Later we discussed the possibilities of a family therapy approach with families from these communities.

The Maori and Pacific Island workers indicated that there would need to be quite a number of changes in process if it were to be effective. They also pointed out that within their own cultures there are therapeutic processes that have existed for many centuries. They wanted to affirm these, and to ensure that the project would be informed by them as well as from the Western body of knowledge. In other words, there was to be an exchange of knowledge. Having established these conditions, we decided to embark on the project together.

Our organisation agreed to make all work associated with a particular culture accountable to the members of staff from that particular community. No work with members of the Samoan community, for example, would be carried out without support and direction from the Samoan consultant. The same was true for the Maori community.

This has resulted in Maori and Samoan workers choosing family therapy approaches which they found helpful for their communities, and applying those aspects in their particular cultural manner, a practice which is acceptable to their people. Their work has moved the resources and skills of family therapy to those communities in need and who were previously denied them. Their cultural patterns of meaning are now embraced in an informed and sensitive manner, such that new threads of resolution and hope are woven successfully with families every day.

Because of these agreements, a 'Just Therapy' has developed, a therapy that is essentially (or simply, or just) about meaning. Because it is about meaning, professional therapists, when working with people from cultures significantly different from their own, are required to defer to key people from those cultures. It is these people who have been tutored in the cultural meaning patterns through their life experience; this knowledge cannot be taught in an academic institution.

The control which key community workers/therapists exert over work with their communities ensures the preservation of their meaning patterns in therapy. It also reverses the institutional imposition of the dominant culture and its meaning patterns, which is at the core of the inequities perpetrated on these people. Furthermore, it is just because therapeutic resources are moved to those groups which are so often denied them.

Finally, the accentuation of cultural meaning and cultural difference also inspires reflection on Western meaning systems and processes. It offers a critical contrast to assess major issues like: co-operation as against individualistic competitive, self-determination; subtle indirect and circular processes of interviewing as opposed to direct and linear ones; traditional spiritual and ecological responses as opposed to a dualistic world view with a separation of physical and spiritual values; and so on. We found that, as a result of this work, we have both identified much more clearly key aspects of Western meaning systems, and received alternative concepts and processes that have informed and improved our therapy with European families.

Socio-economic context

Just as therapy has been presented as intercultural, so it has also been presented as interclass and non-political. Because therapists have pursued sickness in patients rather than the meaning people give to events, their day-to-day living standards, access to housing, employment, income, and so on, have been of little consequence to the 'serious therapeutic task'. This has enabled therapists to side-step all the issues associated with inequity and injustice.

Yet in most modern Western countries those on the lowest 30% of income levels usually experience some of a number of forms of serious deprivation. They may be badly housed, unemployed, or have an inadequate access to money for food, clothing and/or health care. Certain groups of people usually appear in this 30% in disproportionately high numbers when compared with their percentage of the total population. These include women, cultural groups different from the dominant group, and those who are either without jobs or in the lowest paid and most precarious work.

There is ample evidence that the societal health consequences of being part of this group are significant indeed. For example, Harvey Brenner's large scale studies (1973) on the effects of economic recession in the USA, suggested that a 1% rise in unemployment is followed by 6% more first admissions in psychiatric hospitals, a 4% rise in suicides, a 4% increase in state prison admissions, and 6% more homicides. Further research by Brenner (1979) in England and Wales confirmed the American findings.

Abraham Maslow's famous 'hierarchy of needs' (1970) placed shelter, along with food, as one of the basic and fundamental needs which must be met, before any higher needs can be fulfilled. Many people seeking health and welfare resources in our societies have serious housing problems. In an important article entitled 'Housing Poverty in Japan' (1983), Kazuo Hayakawa, a Japanese professor of environmental planning, says:

It is not too much to say that housing is of the greatest importance because it affects the whole of our life in every way; for instance health, security and culture. Children grow up there, family life goes on there, and the greatest part of human life is spent there. Housing is related to human life day in and day out, and is the most important basis for the development of the total human personality in society. (p.298)

In a previous publication we have set out in detail the effects of growing urban poverty in Western countries, and the groups of people that primarily bear the burden (Waldegrave & Coventry 1987). The psychological and physical ill-health that so often accompanies those on low incomes, and those who have only partial access to societies' resources, have been known for years. It is extraordinary that therapy with people whose problems are actually 'the symptoms of poverty' rather than the symptoms of internal family functioning, have been largely carried out using clinical sickness models that do not, of course, address the political meanings of inequity and deprivation.

Those who are employed in a society, for example, are able to participate in the production and services of that society. They have the benefit of earning their money, and the freedom to spend it. As long as they are paid adequately they are able to be, to some considerable extent, self-determining. There is dignity in that.

When a company 'restructures' and lays off a third of its workforce in a city where there is already high unemployment because of the national free market economic policies of their government, then many people are denied participation in the production and services of their society. At the same time they lose a self-determining income, and become the recipients of welfare payments and the associated lowly status. They cease to experience the social contacts they had in the workplace, and their days can become long and pointless as they lose the daily structure the workplace imposed upon their lives.

The loss of dignity is compounded by the guilt of not having a job, and by the contempt of others and comments about 'lazy dole bludgers'. The pressures of family financial needs, and the lure of commercial advertising add to the problem. It is little wonder unemployed people often experience classic depression with feelings of sadness, hopelessness and self-blame. Thus many people in these situations present problems to therapists that in fact are the 'symptoms of poverty'. These may include psychosomatic illnesses, violence, depression, delinquency, psychotic problems, marital stress, truanting, parenting problems, and so on. However, the meaning placed on their experience of events often does not include a political analysis of poverty. On the contrary, they, and many others, consider them to be failures, individually failed. Their feelings of sadness, hopelessness, and self-blame, stem from this problem-centred web of meaning.

If the 'clinical problem' is dealt with in isolation, regardless of the employment context, then the fundamental meaning web will not be addressed. The clinical problem which could be presented as a pervading sense of depression and an accompanying psychosomatic condition, for example, might recede for a time. The meaning that gave rise to the persistent feelings of sadness, hopelessness and self-blame, however, still remains. In a sense, this type of therapy adjusts people to poverty by treating clinical symptoms as though they were simply internal, individual or family problems. The same old web of meaning, together with the political context of unemployment, will soon give rise to the previous manifestation which will provide the fertile environment for new clinical problems. These, of course, will be the new set of symptoms of poverty.

This type of therapy is unjust because it perpetuates the destructive and false myth that unemployed people are the architects of their own destiny. It fails to address the victim nature of unemployment where the economies of today are deregulating, and businesses are restructuring. In most Western countries, regardless of whether all unemployed were highly motivated, well groomed, and relevantly skilled, there just wouldn't be the jobs available for those wanting them. High levels of unemployment have been structured into the economy.

Michele Ritterman (1985) addressed this problem of social context in her work with torture victims and people forced into exile as a result of political decisions in their home country. She says: *The symptom inductive events e.g. the social sequences emanating from a repressive political system – are the opposite of the therapeutic context and the reverse of sequences of healing.* She goes on to say: *We lack a means of assessing the nature of the connection between social context and individual symptoms, a means of assessing the extent to which our social reality builds and develops us or robs us of freedom.* Referring to her therapy with these people, she says: *It seeks to move what has gone inward, becoming a private personal self-absorbed process into a public event of shared social concern. In this way the spell of 'you are damaged' can begin to be broken.*

In many countries, economic planners have sacrificed full employment goals as a trade-off for low inflation. The thousands, and in larger countries millions, who become unemployed as a result of that process, pay a substantial price for the reasonable prosperity of the rest of society. They did not choose this course – they are the casualties thrown up in the big economic game plan; it could be different. These policies are not necessary, as some market economies choose full employment as a central goal of social policy and address inflation in other ways.

The essential political and ethical point is that self-blame and feelings of guilt among unemployed people in such circumstances are as misplaced as those in women who experience the same feelings after they have been beaten up by their partners. A meaning pattern that identifies the generation of the problem internally is ill-informed, and blocks any chance of resolving it. Unemployment and domestic violence require information and understanding of the social context out of which the problems arise. These meanings have to be addressed.

The new threads of meaning remove blame by introducing a more informed analysis of why a person is unemployed. Meanings of self-failure recede, and praise and recognition for the survival strength of the victims are encouraged. The economic and political structures that choose policies that lead to the current lack of employment are identified. So too are organisations of unemployed people and advocacy groups who are working to change those policies. This information strengthens the new pattern of meaning and allows people to choose to work against their economic plight with others if they wish.

Political concepts and clinical concepts are thus drawn together. The problems and 'sicknesses' become identified as the symptoms of unemployment, poverty, and injustice. New meanings that address the clinical factors in a political context emerge. The new understanding strengthens feelings of self-worth and subdues the failure-centred meaning pattern. As the unemployed people have further experiences of 'unsuccessful job interviews', financial constraints, and so on, there is a new meaning context capable of addressing those problems. Instead of experiencing overwhelming feelings of failure, they are able to locate significant aspects of the problems beyond themselves. Their new web of meaning strengthens as they see themselves in context along with thousands and even millions of others in the same situation. Furthermore, they are able to work with others against their experience of injustice if they choose.

In this way, therapists are not making people 'happy in poverty'. On the contrary, the political and economic context is addressed in relation to the problem. Feelings of sadness, hopelessness, and self-blame, transform appropriately to feelings of anger, new possibilities of hope, and self-worth. The loss of motivation, a prime symptom of unemployment, gives way to new energy and adaptability. Those experiencing these problems are then free to direct that energy, having faced their problem openly and in an informed manner.

The onset of many clinically-identified problems for people on low incomes is often associated with socio-economic events. If these problems are isolated from that context and its related meaning, then the therapist has acted politically to silence the voice and understanding of the main victims of inequitable economic policies. Although this may not be what the therapist intended, it is nonetheless usually the effect of their actions.

We believe that therapists in such cases are used (however naively) by the state to mop up the malign consequences of government policies. Making people happy in poverty by treating their clinical problems without reference to their political and economic context ensures that they identify themselves as the problem, thus leaving the state free of blame. It is bewildering that there are still people who consider this sort of therapy is a non-political activity.

We have chosen the structural effects of unemployment to illustrate the significance of socio-economic context to the therapeutic task. We could have chosen bad housing, inadequate incomes, inadequate access to health resources, and so on. The same list of therapeutic problems can be observed as a result of any of these economic situations.

When two or three families are living in a house built for one family, then social, psychological, and physical problems are likely to emerge. Kitchens, hallways, and living rooms double as bedrooms. Insufficient space encourages conflict. It becomes almost impossible for children to study at home after school, and so the problems multiply. Housing is often integrally linked to the therapeutic problems these people present.

The meaning therapists assign to the problem will determine whether or not the problem will continue to be located internally or be defined in terms of its socio-economic context. Either way, therapists act politically. They either address the meanings associated with the society's resource allocation as expressed through their housing and income policies; or, they further entrench feelings of self-blame and internal location of the problem by avoiding it.

Therapists can convey significant political and socio-economic information and meaning: for example, people can be commended for surviving a housing crisis with their family still intact. Their ability to survive a crisis, not of their making but of the housing planners, can be recognised as courageous, committed, or extraordinarily competent. Their failure meanings are challenged as they recognise another authentic way to view the same events. Given the failure of governments to stem the housing crisis among low income families in most Western cities, many people in these situations are directly affected. Furthermore, they can be told they have experienced a gross injustice and survived. We are not sure we would have had the same courage as them had we found ourselves in the same circumstances.

It is our view that good therapy should always be just. The measure of its commitment to justice can be assessed by the commitment to the themes of liberation and self-determination at the heart of the therapeutic process. Denying or simply not addressing the lack of access to survival resources for 20%, and often 30%, of people in Western societies is to deny the influence of these factors on the problems presented in therapy. Such an approach ensures ongoing self-depreciation and dependency.

In order to address the themes of liberation and self-determination, the therapist cannot continue to categorise clinical knowledge separately from cultural, socio-economic, or gender knowledge. The therapist must be informed in all of these areas and ensure that they are included in the therapeutic conversation. They need to be as informed about these as they are about clinical problems and symptoms. In other words, they take a broader, ecological approach to the therapeutic task.

✱   It is also very important that therapists honour the stories of people, particularly those who have been alienated and under-resourced. It is precisely because of the educational, cultural, and other forms of alienation, that relevant therapeutic resources should be available to help reverse the injustice and deal with the cause of many of their problems. Instead of colluding with the system that has mistreated socio-economically deprived people, therapists should facilitate transformation in meanings that will encourage new stories. To this end, family therapists in our organisation are also involved in local community development projects as part of their work.

Two consequences present themselves when therapists choose to work using these beliefs. Firstly, the therapist's conversation involves cultural, socio-economic, and gender-perspective reflections as they relate to the problem. The themes of liberation and self-determination provide the underlying pattern of the therapist's meaning web. The threads they weave convey these implications, while restricting those that convey the internal location of the problem – self-depreciation and dependency. Put another way by White & Epston (1989), clinical problems often refer to 'oppressive or dominant stories and knowledge' which they address by encouraging 're-authoring alternative stories' that by implication are liberating.

Secondly, this ecological approach ensures that therapists become aware of the lack of therapeutic help available for those most in need of health and welfare resources. Therapeutic practice, generally speaking, is concentrated in areas that can be accessed by those who are economically comfortable. In other words, more resources are given to environments of less need. This raises a basic issue of justice itself. Not only has much clinical practice fostered (however unintentionally) the internal location of the problem and dependency among poor people, it has also reduced their access to therapy by the choice of clientele.

Themes of liberation and self-determination in therapy help unmask social myths that condemn the victims of political and economic policies. They encourage openness and the spread of information concerning all the factors that have helped create the problem. They do not protect systems of oppression or deny injustice. They are deeply sensitive to people's most fundamental fears and concerns: for example, the fear parents express when they are not able to provide an adequate home for their children; the fear of increasing debt payments; or the fear of ongoing joblessness. They approach this information with an informed context which facilitates reflection and understanding. ✗

Finally, it may not always be obvious when the socio-economic context is essentially linked to the problem. Levels of poverty and the effects of deprivation are not always easy to define. Furthermore, the problems of the poor are not only products of their socio-economic position. There can be a range of factors that make up their problem-centred pattern. Most importantly, and that which has been the emphasis in this section, is the need for therapists to search for the broader context of the pattern, and where appropriate address it in significant ways.

Gender

The patriarchal structure of modern Western societies has been deeply influenced by the development and persistence of market capitalism. As these societies abandoned subsistent and semi-subsistent local economies, large numbers of people moved from 'the land' to 'the factory' and city. Money became the currency of survival. Now virtually every basic resource, including food, shelter, clothing, medical care, and so on, requires the exchange of money.

As people were increasingly alienated from the land, so also were the families they lived in severed from many of their previous functions as a social institution. These included economic production, responsibility for education, religion, health care, entertainment, and so on. All that was left to the family after the nineteenth and early twentieth century social and economic upheaval was domestic privacy and close interpersonal relationships.

Men, almost entirely, have developed and controlled our modern market-orientated economies. For over two centuries they negotiated a path through scientific research, industrial invention, colonial enterprise (including the slave trade), industrial development, capital expansion, and post-industrial technology. They took control of public life, defining it for themselves, and assigned the private family sphere to women. This division of labour, driven by pervasive economic forces and patriarchal logic, soon became institutionalised. Exceptions to it arose during times of short labour supply, as for example in wartime.

Today the inequities of these developments have been glaringly exposed by feminist critique, and challenged in every aspect of life they have previously influenced. Despite this and the self-determination of many women, Western societies are still largely patriarchal in structure. We have described elsewhere (Waldegrave & Coventry 1987) studies that show men in these societies still capturing and controlling the vast majority of wealth and decision-making, from the boardroom to the local city council. Women earn significantly less than men, and are often economically dependent on them, while the majority of women who live with men and are employed still carry out most of the household domestic responsibilities. The poorest people in Western societies are single parent women. Furthermore, therapists continually see the persistent theme of mothers presiding over private things and fathers presiding over public things, fulfilling the nineteenth century inspired patriarchal division of labour.

Virginia Goldner (1985) notes: *The effect of this dichotomous social arrangement was not only to place women in the home but to virtually equate women with the home, so that women were not simply members of families, they were embodiments of 'The Family'. To use the nineteenth century phrase, the family had become 'women's sphere'. What this means is that family life became female-dominated, a social fact that family therapists mistake for a clinical disturbance. Seen from this perspective, the over-involved mother and peripheral father of the archetypal 'family case' emerge as products of a historical process two hundred years in the making.*

⚡ Feminist therapists and writers have actively addressed issues of gender context in therapy. Marianne Walters, Betty Carter, Peggy Papp, and Olga Silverstein (1988), for example, note: The prevailing patriarchal model of family is grounded in a number of assumptions we have long taken for granted. Basic to patriarchal family organisation is the concept of role complementarity, with instrumental tasks such as earning money through work the province of the male, and emotional tasks such as nurturing, building, and maintaining relationships, and child-rearing the province of the female. In this model, the organisation of power is based on male hierarchy. In contrast to this organisation is our feminist model of family, which is characterised by role symmetry, in which each sex engages in both instrumental and expressive tasks, in both work and nurturing. This model reflects an egalitarian approach to power between male and female, and a *more democratic and consensual approach to parental management of children.*

Referring to their therapeutic approach, they say: *The central operating principles of our revisions of family therapy derive from this feminist perspective. First, no systems formulation can be gender-free. Formulations that purport to be gender-free or 'neutral' are in fact sexist because they reproduce the social pretence that there is equality between men and women. Women, in fact, are disadvantaged in our society, and a failure to acknowledge this fact doubly disadvantages them. Second, all interventions need to take gender into account by recognising the different socialisation processes of women and men, with special attention to the way in which these socialisation processes disadvantage women. We need to recognise that each gender hears a different meaning in the same clinical intervention and accordingly feels either blamed or supported by an identical therapeutic stance.*

These writers articulate very clearly the political implications of gender in therapy, and the meanings therapists ascribe to people. For example, a woman who is seriously depressed and has been threatening physical harm to one of her younger children may be referred to a therapist. The family may have noticed her loss of energy in recent months, her frequent crying, and her unpredictable outbursts. Her husband may have explained to the children that their mother is 'sick' but was receiving help and in time she would get 'better'.

Individual therapeutic work that does not seek out the gender context and meaning associated with it will often entrench the problem further. By defining the woman as 'sick' and treating her in isolation, the meaning passed on to the family and particularly her husband is that they are, by implication, 'well'.

An analysis of family process, however, may reveal the following common scenario, that after some happy and equitable years together, she gave birth to their first child. The father was then assigned the role of breadwinner and her the role of homemaker. Over a period of four years, two other children were born. He became increasingly absent from the home due to work and sporting interests on the weekend, leaving practically all the children's upbringing to her. She felt betrayed and resentful but whenever she wanted to speak about it he either avoided the subject, or listened and didn't do anything.

Over time she grew to expect little affection from her husband and turned to her children for nurturance. This led, on occasions, to her giving mixed messages. At times she would need to discipline but she realised that if she were angry with them she was 'cutting off the hand that was nurturing her'. The children sometimes took advantage of this by playing up and rendering her powerless in her own house. When her husband came home on such occasions he considered the house was in chaos and accused her of failure and loss of control.

In short, her experience in the family was one of failure in marriage and failure in parenthood, both of which she was considered responsible for. Her attempts to address the situation were avoided by her husband. She could not abandon the children so she was locked into a destructive structure which inevitably led to low feelings of depression and other symptomatic behaviour.

It is a travesty of therapy to treat a woman in such circumstances individually and clinically, and then send her back into the family structure that created the problem in the first place. Family members will see her as a 'failed sick mother' whom they have to 'support' on occasions. Her husband's 'strength' will be called upon to help carry the family until she's 'got over this'. He will receive much sympathy for this 'extra load' he's had to 'take on'. She, of course, will become sick again because the underlying inequitable structure that caused the problem has not been addressed.

Therapists who adopt an individual clinical focus in such situations ascribe the symptomatic behaviour to inner personal processes. In doing so, they create a reality that explains to all family members the cause and cure. This profoundly affects the meaning families give to these events and their subsequent behaviour in the future.

Therapists, on the other hand, who are keenly aware of the way socialisation often disadvantages women, will understand the behaviour as a symptom of both the family relationships (as opposed to the individual), and of gender inequity. Therapeutic work with that family will require an analysis of the meaning web that encouraged the development of their family process, and the incorporation of new threads that facilitate new meanings of self-determination among family members through co-operation, sharing, and a liberating approach to gender roles. We are not just referring to a more equitable distribution of household and parenting tasks, but rather a movement from a patriarchal web of meaning to a shared or co-operative meaning structure. Although couples in these situations often stay together, it does not follow that they necessarily will.

This is not simply an argument for family therapy over individual therapy. Family therapy is very often carried out with no reference to gender equity at all. Indeed, the whole concept of 'a family system' with its 'homeostatic balance' and 'a function for every symptom' often 'depoliticises' inequities at the expense of girls and women.

The metaphor of a biological system employed in the majority of family therapy literature may appear appropriate and fitting when referring to school refusal, for example. A therapist might hypothesise that the systemic balancing function of the young person's refusal to go to school is the support of a parent at home who is perceived to be aggrieved and lonely. Therapeutic work might then focus on the resolution of the aggrieved parent and their partner in order to make redundant the balancing behaviour, leaving the young person free to attend school. This is a classical systemic formulation and is attractive because of its functional explanation of the interdependence of family members which removes blame from the person with the problem. The young person is perceived as sensitive and caring, rather than undisciplined and irresponsible.

However, when this same systemic metaphor is used to refer to a man who hits his partner, injustices are likely to occur in therapy. The systemic therapist asks, what is the function of this symptom for the system? In other words, what is the function of violence for this family? To even concede that violence can have a function in a relationship is unjust and outrageous. It suggests a woman is in some way responsible for her partner's violence to her.

The problem with the 'systems' metaphor is that it does not address the power differential between men and women. All behaviour is considered morally relative and all family members contribute to it. Furthermore, the family is often considered self-sufficient and separate from the patriarchal social context, which has spawned violence as a means of control. This can have the effect of removing responsibility from the 'perpetrator' and 'blaming the victim'.

Michelle Bograd (1984) illustrates this with the following sequence: *A wife reminds her husband to fix a broken window; he feels infantilized and withdraws; she impatiently reminds him; he feels inadequate; she demands that he do as he promised; he angrily lashes out and slaps her. In this 'neutral' description, the woman is described as demanding and aggressive, which are conventionally undesirable female qualities. Her behaviour is framed as provocation or nagging, and not as the legitimate right of a wife to voice dissatisfaction. The husband's role is downplayed through the more sympathic portrayal of his insecurity. His violence is almost normalised as an understandable attempt to regain his 'rightful' place in the marriage. Similar formulations are further biased against women because they: 1) imply that the battered woman could and should control her husband's feelings and actions; 2) attenuate (reduce) the man's responsibility for his violence; 3) ignore physical size differences between men and women; and 4) deny that violence may be linked to pre-existing personality characteristics of the abusive husband and not only to transactional variables that developed over the course of the relationship.*

If the patriarchal web of meaning that enabled and to some extent justified the violence is not addressed, then, even though the hitting may stop, new controlling behaviours are likely to emerge.

Patriarchy refers to a view of the right to power dominance by men over women at every level of society from government to the family. It is integrally woven into the structures of modern Western societies (and most others as well) and all its institutions. It is inequitable and unjust, and any therapy which does not address that injustice consciously is by implication sexist.

Constructivist approaches to family therapy can fall into the same trap as the systemic approach. The realities created by both family members and therapists are viewed as interpretive observer descriptions, each carrying their own meaning. The denial of objective reality in these observer descriptions can lead therapists to treat the attributions of meaning given by different family members as being of equal value. The stories of abused children and women, however, are more likely to reflect what really happens in a household, than the reduced story a person who abuses often gives.

The moral relativism latent in the constructivist approach fails to identify the preferable or even the malign meaning webs intrinsic to such therapy situations. In other words, this approach de-politicises the broader social context and inequities. Issues of responsibility and blame are critical in abuse work. Abusive behaviour and the patriarchal meanings central to its creation need to be opposed, and abused people relieved of blame. A construction that acknowledges the gender context is an ethically preferable construction, as the political meanings are woven into the clinical process.

The manner in which therapists seek information concerning the problem in therapy will also convey meaning, and determine the sort of information they will receive from people. If a therapist considers the family to be a social institution that protects and encourages intimacy, for example, then they may well question the need for an adult member to stay in that family when, despite numerous attempts to address the problem, processes in the family destroy intimacy. If, on the other hand, a therapist considers that families should usually be helped to stay together, they will tend not to raise such questions.

The avoidance of key questions limits therapy to the existing family structures. Where inequities are occurring within the family, the total therapeutic process may only serve to enshrine patriarchal meanings and practices. However, questions concerning the choice people have to continue to live together, the economic possibilities of separation, the possibilities and fears of violence if a woman chooses to leave, and the shared issues of emotional and psychological dependence can open discussion enabling choice, change, and bargaining between them. Thus the process is enlarged and new possibilities of self-determination, hope, and resolution are facilitated.

Other modes of questioning can help people reflect on patriarchal meaning webs in their family during the process of therapy. McKinnon & Miller suggest:

Such questions as: 'Who has been most influential in determining current beliefs? Who is most served by the current beliefs and social definitions of problems and relationships? What has been the socio-historical evolution of these beliefs?' (These questions can be simplified.) This, by necessity takes us beyond the family as a thing and forces us to examine the social construction of our own theories and of ideologies concerning the family, gender, heterosexuality, motherhood, childhood, and of problems we have hitherto located within the family such as child abuse, incest and wife battering. (1987)

Questioning that broadens the therapeutic discussion to the webs of meaning underlying and surrounding behaviour admits the possibility of changes of meaning. Certain other questions, phrases, and themes in therapy can restrict that possibility. The use of phrases like a 'violent family', when referring to a family where a father is violent, confuses responsibility and meaning. The term 'sexual addict' instead of 'sexual abuser' changes a political metaphor into a medical one, and reduces responsibility. Likewise, the common practice of working for change in the family via the most responsive person, usually the mother, simply plays into the old patriarchal meaning web. She ends up having to do most of the work and take most of the responsibility.

Work against patriarchy requires continual monitoring, because therapists have grown up socially gendered like their clients. In our organisation, oversight of this work is carried out by the women therapists. Over time, appropriate gender roles have been allocated to the various therapists. When a woman has been abused, for example, she is seen by another woman, and the man who abused her is seen by a man. It is only after he has taken responsibility for his abuse that we will engage in a family interview. We ensure that our staff complement includes at least one man and one woman from each of the three cultures we work in partnership with. For men who are violent we also run culturally-based groups directed towards non-violence.

One recent example of this gender related approach was our attempt, after years of work with both the victim/survivors and perpetrators of violence, to articulate a further revised set of policy guidelines for therapists working with men who abuse. We were trying to address the problem therapists experience as they work beside a person who abuses. On occasions they can advocate on his behalf and resist challenging directly his violent behaviour.

Early on in this project we agreed that men working with those who abuse should make their therapy accountable in a direct way to women workers in the agency. Various gatherings have been called over the years as our reflections on the work have matured. The most recent meeting articulated the following policy goals which were subsequently adopted by the whole agency.

When working with men who abuse

Men's stories should not be told in a vacuum. Reflective work with their stories should help them identify the growth and persistence of abuse.

- Work should primarily focus on the abuse and its consequences on the women and/or other victims and their liberation, and secondarily on the victim experience of the person who abuses, e.g. racism, problem childhood, etc.

The test of good work is a change of heart or second order change, that internalises the issues set out in (1) and (2) above. This is beyond simple intellectual or intentional change.

- When working together, male workers share the story as the person who abuses tells it. Female workers share the story as the abused person tells it. It should be recognised that the stories of people who abuse usually reduce the level of abuse, and male workers should not advocate against the story of the person who has been abused.

- Within the context of a warm, working relationship, male workers need to be direct, challenging, very clear on the issues of oppressive violence, and professional in their work with abusers.

- Confidentiality remains with the agency and the normal procedures that are in place for implementing this. Information from the female workers, in particular, is not to be shared with the person who abuses, without permission from that female worker. A similar procedure should also occur with information given by male workers.

This policy clarifies a preferential meaning web with regard to one therapeutic area. Therapists who agree to this set of guidelines have chosen a pattern of values that are opposed to the continuation of patriarchal webs of meaning. Furthermore, the relationship between male and female therapists is woven into the policy.

This approach directly affects the therapeutic task. The meaning that is created by the therapist becomes apparent within the context of the policy guidelines. Furthermore, this offers a well-grounded structure for appropriate accountability between colleagues.

Gender equity is a just expectation of any therapist and their work. For it to be realised, the broader patriarchal structures of society should be addressed in our therapy, our organisations, and our practice. The structures of Western societies are not gender-free, nor is any therapeutic work. We contend that therapists should work for equality between men and women by recognising the current gender injustices, and consciously creating therapies that facilitate new meanings that will enable equality in relationships.

The therapeutic exchange

Therapy, in our view, essentially involves an energised conversation, during which the therapist listens respectfully for the articulation of meaning by a person or a family. Professionalism, with this approach, is judged by the quality and skills of the conversation, rather than superior knowledge and training. The skilled therapist helps people to experience new ways of reflecting on, and organising, the significance they give events. The domination of the problem-focussed web of meaning becomes addressed by them as they weave new threads of possibilities.

This approach imparts to those coming for therapy a sense of prominence. Their story is the focus of therapy, and they are perceived by the therapist to be the experts in articulating its significance and meaning. The therapist's contribution is to honour the story presented in therapy, by encouraging its articulation, and respecting its significance for the people concerned. The therapist then offers new meanings and possibilities of resolution and hope from the same events.

From this perspective the so-called 'presenting problem' is not a pathology to be treated, but a sacred story given in trust. People come to therapy and make themselves vulnerable by exposing the deepest and most personal events in their lives, along with their explanations of those events. They often feel defeated and even humiliated by the persistence of their problem. In these circumstances their exposing of their pain and the context out of which it springs, is like a gift, a very personal offering, to the therapist: it has a spiritual quality.

This offering is worthy of honour. It is not a scientific pathology that requires removal, nor is it an ill-informed understanding of the problem that requires correction. It is, rather, a person's articulation of events and the meaning given to those events which have become problematic. The story needs to be respected in a manner not dissimilar from that of a trusting friend exposing their own pain or sorrow. Help is often needed in describing it – to include parts forgotten or difficult to mention, and finally to reflect on it.

It follows from this approach that a therapist of the same culture as the client's will more easily understand the significance given in a story. They will also be more informed about possible new meanings ascribed to those same events, drawing significantly on the culture, rather than disturbing and alienating it. That expertise is at least as significant as professional clinical knowledge, and in some cases more so.

This approach offers the possibility of cultural partnerships in therapy, with Black, Hispanic or Indian cultures in the United States, for example, or Maori and Pacific Island in New Zealand. The cultural expert, whom we refer to as a 'cultural consultant', offers understanding concerning meaning, and the clinical expert offers understanding concerning the Western body of psychological knowledge. As long as the expertise of both is respected equally, the cultural consultant will, over time, learn clinical knowledge, and the clinical consultant will learn sensitivity and differences in cultural terms.

In this manner, cultural groups who have little access to therapeutic resources see members of their community respected and trained in therapy. Furthermore, the expertise of the cultural consultant appropriately deters the clinical consultant from intercultural ascriptions of meaning. The particular meaning systems of the particular cultural group then become increasingly differentiated from the dominant meaning systems. Eventually the cultural consultant becomes clinical and cultural consultant. As is sometimes said in New Zealand: *A Maori can always learn to be a psychologist, but a psychologist cannot learn to be Maori.* And we could add, *but a psychologist can learn to respect and be sensitive to things Maori, or Samoan, or Black, or Hispanic, or Australian Aboriginal, and so on.*

Women therapists also have experiences and understanding in common that are differentiated from those of men. Their therapeutic attentiveness to women's story in therapy, and their analysis of appropriate new meaning, is transforming modern approaches. The field in the past has been dominated by male theorists whose meaning systems have grown largely out of patriarchal societies and scientific discipline. There are numerous therapeutic occasions where women are simply more capable, more appropriate and more expert than men. They can relate to, and listen for, the articulation of meaning more easily because it is closer to their own.

Therapists then, initiate conversation in the first interview. Their demeanour, their words, and their attitude communicate meaning immediately. Different cultures, for example, have ways of beginning conversations with those they haven't met before, and people from the same culture know at the outset if their processes are going to be understood and respected. A Maori family in New Zealand will feel much more comfortable, if each person is introduced and the therapist shakes hands individually, or hongi (press noses respectfully), or kisses the women on the side of the cheek. After this people will sit down and the conversation will focus on where they come from, who their family are related to, and connections that may exist between the therapist and any members of the extended family. It is only after this process, and other similar discussions, that it becomes appropriate to introduce the reasons for coming to therapy.

People struggling to survive economically soon know whether their daily pain is appreciated and understood. Therapists who usually experience much more comfortable economic circumstances express their reality by the way they talk and the significance they give to the struggles of poor people. Can they identify with the toughness that life in poverty requires of families? Can they link into the humour? Do their comments reflect establishment views that denigrate poor people, or do they respect their stories?

We begin the interview informally in a manner that attempts to relax the people while giving an underlying message of respect and genuine interest in them and what they care about. We then seek to draw out their story. It is very important that it is their story, without intrusion or contamination by the therapist. We elicit this with a very straightforward and open question, like:
- *Well, what's brought you along here today?* or
- *What is it that you would like from us?* or
- *Okay, perhaps you could tell me what the problem is?*

By asking this kind of question, the therapist throws the initiative over to the person/people to define the problem, explain the significance and set the goals of the therapeutic partnership. They tell their story and, regardless of what they say, it is taken very seriously. The therapist does not define the order of the speakers or direct the discussion. Instead s/he allows the process to shape itself.

When working with families, the spokespersons, the silent ones, the conflicts, the partnerships, and the articulations are all observed. Some families volunteer the story and articulate detail with very little prompting from the therapist. Others elaborate with the help of enquiring questions to give details, place events in sequence and, with encouragement, discuss those things they find difficult to say.

The therapist's task is to draw out the story and observe the meaning the family gives to the story. S/he should not advise, interpret, congratulate, or in any way interfere with the people's story. The therapist's task is to draw it out, take it seriously, and communicate respect, understanding, and concern.

By comparison with many other therapies, the therapist practising this approach is verbally inactive. Their speaking simply acts to facilitate and promote maximum relevant detail relating to the person/people's story. They usually contribute only about 10% to 20% of the therapeutic conversation. Every question is carefully phrased to encourage the articulation of events and the meaning the family ascribes to those events.

Although the questioning is open-ended in an attempt not to 'lead' the people, the information sought is deliberately chosen. We ask questions that bring out gender, cultural and socio-economic contexts and meanings. We are interested in how other members of the family, and extended family, reacted, who they went to for advice, what reason they give for such-and-such an event, what is their understanding of what happened, what significance they give these events, and so on. The answers to these types of questions convey the gender, socio-economic and cultural ascriptions of meaning conveyed by people.

It is very important that the questioner seeks to clarify and understand, while never on any occasion assuming or predicting people's responses. S/he asks many 'what' questions and 'how' questions, for example:

- *How old were you at this time? What do you think of the teacher's explanation?*

- *What did you do when she said she was going to kill herself? So he hid in the cupboard, then what happened? How often does he hit you?*

'What' and 'how' questions invite raw information. The therapist is asked to avoid 'why' questions which invite a thinking interpretation of the raw material. The description of events are already usually organised by people into some primary-meaning web. Further interpretations tend to obscure its simplicity and energy. If the meaning of an event is not clear, we encourage a 'what framework' for a 'why' type question, e.g. *What explanation would you give for Johnny's disappearance?*

Other 'what' type questions can be used without the use of the words 'what' and 'how', e.g. *Where were you living at that time? Did you get on okay with your father then? Who was it that took you to hospital?*

The story being told can also be prompted by emphasising or repeating key phrases said by that person during therapy as an invitation to expand, for example: Jane: *My parents resented me.* Therapist: *They resented you?* Jane: *Yeah, they always ...*

The therapist persists with the family to enable their story to be recounted in full and an account of the meanings they attribute to it to be given. If there are connections that are not understood, further questions elicit the information. It is never assumed. If parts of the story are unclear, questions to clarify are asked. If other parts are difficult to speak about, support is given to encourage their articulation.

This process encourages people to own their stories and promote them as the focus of therapy. This not only provides the information the therapist requires to address the problem appropriately, it also gives a considerable measure of control of the therapeutic conversation over to the clients. Their stories and points-of-view are requested, and taken seriously.

For some clients this is not always easy, especially when the person is in a low functioning state. On these occasions the therapist needs to engage verbally more frequently. The following dialogue occurred in the first interview I had with the family I referred to earlier, where Rick, the father and husband, had spent a year in two psychiatric hospitals:

Therapist: *I need to know if there's anything you want from us.*

Rick: *Well, I want to try and get better.*

Therapist: (gently) *Better from what? I don't really know what is your problem.*

Rick: *I get depression.*

Therapist: *It's a pretty wide term. What do you mean by that?*

Rick: *Well, I just seem to have it in me all the time.*

Therapist: *You have it in you?*

Rick: *Mmmm.*

Therapist: *How do you know you've got it? What is it that's depressed?*

(silence)

Rick: *I don't know really.*

Therapist: *So, you've got depression in you but you don't know what's depressed. Do you have any feeling? Do you have any thoughts?*

Coming from an institution that both defined and acted for him, it was important to signal that he needed to clarify his own problem and that we would treat that very seriously. Later:

Therapist: *I'm not always sure the way other people describe it is the accurate way. Now, we've had some indication from the hospital of what they think, but for us it's much more important to get it from you because you're the one that lives with it.*

Rick: *Yeah.*

Therapist: *They don't. I don't. It's something you're living with, and your family lives with it.*

Rick: *Yeah.*

Therapist: *So, I'm really interested in the way you see it, your definition of it. I mean, how does it affect you? Can you just sort of put some words around it?*

Rick: *Well, it gives me no energy and that.*

Therapist: *No energy ... You just feel all tired or something. Is that something different from the way you used to feel?*

Rick: *Yeah.*

Therapist: *How did you used to feel?*

Rick: *Good as gold.*

Therapist: *Good as gold?*

Rick: *Yeah.*

Later, to the wife and mother in the family:

Therapist: *What do you observe happens to Rick when he gets depressed?*

Sharon: *Um, he finds it hard, difficult to talk. Um, and there is sort of no feeling, or no emotions. There hasn't been any of that for months.*

Therapist: *No feelings, no emotions?* (To Rick) *Is that the way you feel?*

Rick: *Yes.*

Therapist: *You don't have any feelings at all?*

Rick: *No.*

Therapist: *Gees, that's a bit rough, eh? Do you ever feel happy at all, or do you always feel bad?*

Rick: *I always feel down to it.*

Therapist: *Alright.* (To Sharon) *And there's not much talking?*

Sharon: *No.*

It was also important to know the children's experience. I later enquired of the ten-year-old son and brother:

Therapist: *Do you know what your dad is talking about when he says he gets depressed? Do you know what he means?*

Guy: *No, not really.*

Therapist: *No ... Do you notice anything different about your dad?*

Guy: *Yeah, it's hard to talk.*

Therapist: *Hard to talk?*

Guy: *Yeah, or make a conversation.*

Therapist: *Did you used to talk to him much more?*

Guy: *Yeah, we used to play with him. We miss that now.*

Therapist: *Oh, he doesn't play so much?*

Guy: *No he can't, really.*

In a sense, this dialogue is atypical because the therapist is much more involved than usual in the verbal interplay. In most circumstances one or two questions initiate a story from people. When that is not forthcoming, because of, as in this instance, the very low functioning state of the person, then the story is elicited with more verbal participation by the therapist. The focus remains on 'what' type questions, people's experience, and the meaning they give to that experience. The therapist often recycles phrases used by the family for further clarification and amplification. This indicates to the family both attentiveness and interest on the part of the therapist.

This process of storytelling and questioning usually takes us about 50 minutes to an hour. The therapist then leaves the people to reflect, either by themselves, or preferably with a colleague, who has been observing the interview through reflective glass. (The family, of course, met the observer before the interview began and were aware they were being 'screened'.)

An analysis of the problem-centred story then takes place. There are obvious advantages if the therapist has an observer to reflect with. Together they note the events referred to in the story and the meaning ascribed by different members to those events. They discuss the emergence and development of the problem into its central, dominating focus.

Because culture, gender and socio-economic context are at the heart of people's experience and the development of their meaning webs, therapists appropriate to the particular context are assigned to the persons or families coming for therapy. Male and female therapists, for example, have particular roles when gender issues are central to the problem. When the clients come from cultures that are significantly different from the majority culture, and are dominated in society, therapists belonging to those cultures take the leading role. These therapists more easily understand the meaning webs, and know better how to strengthen people by encouraging them within the context of their culture, rather than alienating them from it.

Using the information gained, the therapists then create alternative meaning that will enable resolution and hope from the events previously described by the family. They prepare a message or reflection for the family or person which is designed to weave new threads of meaning that will undo the rigid problem-centred pattern.

The process takes about a quarter of an hour to twenty minutes. Meanwhile, the family chatter, drink coffee, and relax. The therapist who has been visible throughout the story session then returns to the family with a reflective message, in note form or the full text. The earlier process of listening to, and drawing out the people's story is reversed. Instead, they listen to the message from the therapist, which is read twice, preferably in silence (though it's not always possible).

The interview finishes after the message. The message is not designed to be discussed at this point; instead it is designed to arrest the domination of the problem by the surprising appearance of an alternative creation of reality around the same events. The new reality loosens the threads of the old pattern and sensationally opens the design to new possibilities.

An illustration of the sort of message we give is taken from a Samoan family with whom we worked. The Department of Social Welfare referred the family because of their concern about James who, at the age of 14, had been assigned by the court to a Department children's home. The parents, Samu and Sieni, were charged by the police with not having James 'under proper care and control'. James had been living on the streets, truanting from school, and had been caught breaking and entering a number of local businesses during the evenings. James' father, Samu, believed in very strong physical punishment when disciplining his children. He was an ex-boxer and had punished his children severely in the past. He was also in the habit of drinking a lot and scaring Sieni and the children when he came home. There were two girls still living at home. The Departmental workers felt they were unable to communicate with the family at all. We were approached because of the Samoan workers in our organisation.

Two Samoan women and I were involved in the therapy. One of the women was in the room with the family and the other two of us were behind the one-way screen. At the end of the first interview the therapist read the following message twice:

The team has listened very closely to all the things that you have said. They were very moved by your honesty and your openness, and by your tears of pain. As a family you have had hard times but they know that you have already started to change these, and you want to find love and happiness again together.

Samu, the team knows how important it is for you to have a good family name. They also know that some of your children have hurt you. You have thought about this a lot and have tried to make some changes to help all your family. Not only have you tried to get James to be good and to do what you

want him to do, but you have also cut down a lot of your own drinking for the
sake of your kids and your family. The team were really happy that you have
made these changes.

Sieni, the team understood how much you care for all your children and
your husband. They thought you were a hard-working good mother who
prays for all her children. They know that you have reached the point of
nearly giving up with James at times, but you are still here with your family
because you wanted to know what to do best for them.

James, the team know that even though you want to be with your mates a
lot, you have chosen 'to come home and belong to your family'. You have
already begun to try to get things right and they know you will go on trying.
The team thinks you love your father very much. They saw how afraid you got
when he became drunk, in case he was mugged, the way some street kids mug
other drunk people.

Winnie and Anne, the team could tell that you cared a lot for your family
and want things to come right. Your tears, Winnie, showed us your love.

As a family, you still have some problems. The changes that have taken
place will need to go on. And some of you in the family seem to be quite
lonely. We think that you have enough alofa [a Samoan word that refers to
very deep, committed, and sacrificial love] *and strength in your family to*
make these problems come right and be happy, with some help from all of us
working together.

The message was designed to present a different reality around the same
events the family had experienced. Essentially, the family, which was proudly
Samoan, had been humiliated by being taken to court and having their child
assigned to a State Home, The court system categorised both the parents as being
inadequate for the task. The Department viewed them as another failed family.
The parents, who were poor immigrants, were bringing up their children as they
would in Samoa, where housing is in extended family structures that are open to
the whole village. The children had quickly adapted from the traditional
processes in Samoa to the less defined ones in New Zealand, while their parents
were still struggling with speaking English. They were living in one of the
poorest suburbs in the Wellington region. Their situation was not dissimilar to
that of numbers of Pacific Island immigrant families in New Zealand.

The message (perhaps surprisingly) indicated that we considered the parents were both competent and committed to their children, and that the children loved their parents. Furthermore, there was enough alofa and strength in the family to see them through these difficult times. We recognised deep Samoan values, such as concern for a 'good family name', our description of 'a good mother who prays for all her children' and 'alofa'. We acknowledged the family's pain, and the gift of their openness to us, particularly after their distrust of the Department of Social Welfare.

Each person and their particular loneliness was addressed. The parents struggled with English which was their second language, so we used simple concepts like being 'happy' and being 'good', and so on. Nevertheless, all the information we gave back to the family was assembled from the story they had told us.

Because the message was an authentic creation that viewed the same events from a different perspective, it loosened the tightly woven pattern of failure, humiliation, and incompetence. While our meaning respected the family's efforts and acknowledged their pain, the new information imparted to them was surprising and stunning! Its impact was increased by reversing the interview structure from the family's articulation of their story, to our reflection on those same events. In this manner we began to weave the new threads of resolution and hope.

We consider that the real work of therapy takes place in people's lives between interviews. We don't give the message for debate; instead we offer a dynamic reflection, that is designed to impact on the problem-centred meaning web that organises people's creation of reality. Its significance unravels slowly in the days following, as people view their lives and relationships differently.

Each interview after the first simply pursues the development of meaning among the family. After pleasantries and any appropriate acknowledgements, we ask another open-ended question like:
-   *How have things been since we last saw you?*
-   *What's happened since we last saw you?*

Again the therapist persistently tracks events and the meaning given to events with 'what' and 'how' type questions.

During the interview, all, or as many as possible, of the critical problem areas are tracked in the family's story. The therapist monitors the movement in these areas. The stories change over time as the threads of new meaning emerge. The therapist, generally speaking, continues to contribute only 10% to 20% of the verbal interplay as s/he draws experience and meaning from the family.

After the first interview it is very important to highlight the differences in meaning and behaviour which have emerged since earlier interviews. These changes are not congratulated or marvelled upon; they are simply noted as different from last time. Congratulations are offered later in the message to increase its impact. Underlining change simply involves a statement like:

- *Well, that's different from what was happening last time, isn't it? So you've decided to trust your parents now? Okay, what was it like when you did that?...*

and the therapist tracks the new information, or

- *Gee, that's a change, eh. And what happened after that?*

The messages given from the second interview onwards begin by noting the changes in behaviour and meaning since the previous interview. They go on to spell out the significance the therapists give to certain key behaviours that have occurred between interviews. The message has great flexibility: information can be presented in an encouraging manner, a directive educational manner, in paradoxical form, in dilemma form, or in whatever way the therapist thinks will loosen the old threads of meaning and encourage growth of the new ones.

The message at the end of the second interview with the family we have just referred to, for example, took the following form:

The team has been very impressed with all the changes that have occurred in your family since they last saw you.

Sieni, the team noted that you have decided to trust your children more. You are letting them take care of themselves more as they grow up. They know that you know that if you and Samu trust them then, they are more likely to be responsible for themselves. They heard you say how very proud about your kids you are. They also wanted you to know that they understood how you have been hurt in the past by Samu and still have to talk about that at times like this. Despite all these things, you still love him and your family very much and that is why you are still with them.

Samu, the team have heard today from you, and all the members of your family, about your changes. They know that you know just how dangerous your drinking has been to the family. Your family can smile again now that you don't come home drunk. Because you have succeeded in this, your children and your wife are not afraid of you like they used to be. They want to talk with you now. The team was very impressed with the way you did not interrupt Sieni to defend yourself when she wanted to talk about those bad times from the past. They think the most important thing you said today was near the end when you said 'Now I don't *want to give a hiding, I* want *to talk'. They thought that was wonderful. Winnie and James, we know it's been a long time for you here today, but we think you understand that these times help make things for your family better. The team thinks you must really love your parents very much, both mother and father, because you have begun to speak more freely with them very quickly. As they have trusted you and let you go out, you have stopped being afraid and got closer to them. You are beginning to trust each other. And the team knows that all of you know that this is the start of good and happy family life.*

The team understands that the court case next Monday is a worry for you. They want to say that they think that you are making the right preparations for a new beginning as a family together. They think you can begin to feel confident and sure about the future.

In a culturally appropriate way, this message respectfully placed the initiative with the parents, who had decided to trust their children in a more risky manner. As a result, the children had responded with closeness and trust themselves. In this way, the clear boundaries of respect and status between parents and children in Samoan families were not disturbed. Trust and responsibility were linked, enabling the parents to adapt to the more liberal pressures on their children in New Zealand, while at the same time encouraging them to understand that this placed some form of appropriate accountability upon the children.

The message also addressed key gender issues in the family. The therapist had drawn from Sieni during the interview, articulation of her deep hurt and distrust of Samu because of his drinking and violence. In the message she was spoken to first, and the legitimacy of her pain acknowledged. Samu was directly reminded how dangerous his behaviour was, and his determination to change his ways was quoted. The word 'brave' that is often associated with male violence, was re-interpreted to refer to him humbly listening, without defending himself, to Sieni's talk about the bad tunes.

All of this was carefully expressed with hope and respect for the family.

Each paragraph attempted to strengthen the meanings that were encouraging the new behaviour. As with the first interview, all subsequent messages were read twice.

We only needed to see this family over four interviews. The Department of Social Welfare and the Judge then assessed the family home as being the most appropriate place for James to live. This was because parents and children were trusting each other and the violence and alcohol abuse had ceased. As the Department's report put it:

> *Overall, it would appear that movement has taken place and there is a far greater match in ideas and expectations of discipline and boundaries between parents and children in this family. Parents and children are also communicating more freely and discussion is being seen as a good method of problem solving. Furthermore, the family home was the place James now wanted to live in.*

By addressing the meaning web in this way, a poor, immigrant, broken family, enmeshed in police, judicial, and welfare systems, reassessed and liberated themselves from those systems, becoming self-determining after only four sessions.

Another example of this process is offered via the messages given at the end of the first and fourth interviews with a family in which life-threatening violence had occurred on numerous occasions. The mother, Mere, and her two sons, George and Raymond, were referred to our centre by the local women's refuge. Mere had been seriously beaten on many occasions and taken to hospital with head injuries and broken bones. It was considered too dangerous for her to stay in the local women's refuge in her town so she was moved to our area. She left behind her husband and elder son. In the refuge her younger 8 year old son, Raymond, was causing havoc for the other families. He was switching the channels on the only TV set while others were watching a program, hitting other children in the refuge, being very rude to his mother and continually making a lot of noise around the other families.

The family was Maori and a Maori woman therapist and I worked with them. She was the therapist in the room. At the end of the first interview we compiled the following message:

We'd like to congratulate you, Mere, for putting an end to the cycle of violence. It takes a lot of courage to leave your home town, and Jim and Pete. We can see you are determined to make a new life, and we think you are a very responsible mother. George and Raymond, we think you are very lucky to have a mother who loves you the way she does; a mother who has got the courage to make a new start.

George – we know that you support your mother a lot, but we are worried, Raymond, that you are acting more like a six-year-old than an eight-year-old. Eight-year-olds are usually smart enough to know that when they live with other people they should respect *them by being quiet and helpful. Young kids like six-year-olds make a lot of noise, show off, and like hitting small children. They like hitting their mothers and switching TV programs. Six-year-olds are too dumb to know how to respect people around them, especially adults.*

We want you to grow up to be an eight-year-old. You can learn from your brother how to quieten down, not show off, and respect *your mother like an older kid. We know that you can. You don't have to be six.*

The message was designed to recognise Mere's courage and strength, and to set that meaning alongside her very depressed and hopeless feelings of failure. Again, we acknowledged her self-determining steps 'to end the cycle of violence'. It is not always appropriate in Maori culture to praise someone directly: they can often feel very embarrassed. Instead we told George and Raymond how lucky they were to have a mother like her. This indirect message was both culturally appropriate and gender sensitive. The boys, particularly Raymond, were still confused as to the rights and wrongs of their mother's move.

The words to Raymond also illustrated ways of affecting meaning change in children. He thought all his antisocial behaviour was a sign of his maturity and future manhood. By redefining age and maturity in a manner that seduced him, we offered another perspective designed to stun and arrest his current behaviour and beliefs. By repeating the word 'respect', we were calling on a deep Maori value which he would have heard many times.

Raymond's response was immediate and dramatic. Mere soon moved into her own house. The message at the end of the fourth and last interview tells the story, and continues our appreciation of Mere's ability and courage. By this time we had got to know her a lot better, and we thought she should receive our praise both directly and indirectly without embarrassment:

Mere, we are very impressed with the way you have been able to take charge of your family and make your boys and yourself safe. You now have an independent life and your boys look good.

George and Raymond, you have a wonderful mother who has made big changes in her life so that you can all be happy. She has courage, strength, and a lot of aroha (a Maori word that refers to very deep, committed, and sacrificial love). *We are also very impressed with you kids. We could hardly believe, Raymond, that you are the same boy that came here three months ago, who is now getting achievement awards at school. You've done very well indeed, and George, you've also been very good and we wish you a lot of luck on your rugby trip to Australia.*

Mere, you've done very well. You are now communicating with your kids. You sit down and talk, and you have a peaceful house to live in. They look so much better.

You must be very careful in the future never to get involved where there is violence. Do not let a lot of people you are not sure about into your house. Set the controls yourself. You are independent now and you must be very careful not to get into a relationship where there is violence again.

Central to this approach to therapy is a radical juxtaposition of the lengthy and detailed focus on the people's story with the trance-like, brief and positive reflection of the therapists. The new and contrasting meaning will only be adopted, of course, if it springs authentically from the detailed information given by them. Because the person or family has been carefully listened to, they tend to be very responsive to the therapist's reflection. They often lean forward when the therapist comes in with the message and are usually exceedingly attentive.

In some clinical circles, messages have been used in an ill-considered manner – as authoritative interventions. It should be clear from the explanations and examples given here that we prepare sensitive messages only after prolonged attentive reflection on people's stories of pain. They are designed to free them from the rigidity of problem-focussed meaning, and lead them to liberating and self-determining possibilities. The new meanings are profoundly ethical because, as we have explained, the context is based upon just principles.

The therapist in the room is not interrupted by the observing therapist, unless the need is felt to change direction or seek further information. Often there is no interruption at all. Too many disrupt the story and its flow.

The real work is carried out rapidly after the story focus, and before the message is given. The observing therapist can be very helpful here. It is the colloquial but cleverly devised response of the therapists that creates surprise and initiates change. Practice speeds this process up. We usually take about 15 minutes to compile the message, but it can vary from between 10 and 20 minutes.

The language used both in questioning and in the message is colloquial, rather than literary. It is designed to re-echo phrases used by those people in therapy. The linguistic precision increases with experience, and its use is essential when creating new and positive patterns out of the old problem-centred ones. Key words provide the bridge from the old concept to the new ones.

Visitors often refer to our reflective messages as 'interventions' and 'reframes'. We don't like those metaphors, for the same reason (as we noted earlier) we disliked use of the term 'constructivism'. These controlling and mechanical metaphors don't indicate the sensitivity of the therapeutic exchange. Furthermore, these messages are not simple reframes, but rather changes in total patterns of meaning.

Our approach enables a thorough exploration of these patterns and their changes through therapy. The apparent simplicity of the approach should not be confused with a lack of professionalism or reduction of clinical expertise. On the contrary, the messages require creative and lateral thinking skills that are developed over years. We believe that people's webs of meaning lie at the heart of the change that occurs in the process of therapy. The messages endeavour to capture the essence of that.

It should also be noted that variations on the message can be made, especially during later interviews. For example, it can come halfway through an interview, if it seems an appropriate time for discussion; instead of the usual reflection, a metaphorical story can be very effectively told. In addition, a team split can take place to emphasise a dilemma where the person in front predicts or recommends one set of actions and while the one behind offers the opposite, thus leaving the person or family with both viewpoints to reflect on – and so on. As we have already noted, messages can also carry significant political, cultural, or social information and meaning.

People with cultural knowledge or community skills can be trained in this approach. The continual experience of analysing, reflecting with an experienced therapist as the message is prepared is a rich learning opportunity. If the person is also reading and discussing a breadth of clinical knowledge, he or she can soon become an effective therapist. Those who are normally denied access to therapeutic training, because of a lack of academic requirements, can become good therapists, working in particular with people from their own community. We have trained numbers of people like this.

The therapy, we think, is just. It is just because it requires the gender, cultural, and socio-economic contexts to be taken seriously. These issues are integral to the therapy. It is also just because it gets to the simple heart of therapeutic change, and enables a broader range of people to become therapists, particularly those from groups who have previously been denied that opportunity. It does so without compromising skill, knowledge, or effective change. Finally, it is just therapy – a seemingly straightforward approach to complex problems.

References

Bateson, G. 1972: *Steps to an Ecology of Mind.* New York: Ballantine Books.

Bateson, G. 1980: *Mind and Nature: A necessary unity.* New York: Bantam Books.

Boyd-Franklin, N. 1989: *Black Families in Therapy: A multisystems approach.* New York: Guilford.

Brenner, M.H. 1973: *Mental Illness and the Economy.* Harvard University.

Brenner, M.H. 1979: 'Mortality and the national economy: A review and the experience of England and Wales 1936-76.' *Lancet*, 15:568-573.

Bograd, M. 1984: 'Family systems approach to wife battering: A feminist critique.' *American Journal of Orthopsychiatry*, 54(4):558-568.

Epston, D. & White, M. 1989: *Literate Means to Therapeutic Ends.* Adelaide: Dulwich Centre Publications.

Goldner, V. 1985: 'Feminism and family therapy.' *Family Process*, 24:31-47.

Hayakawa, K. 1983: 'Housing poverty in Japan.' *Ekistics*, Jan/Feb.

McGoldrick, M., Pearce, J.K. & Giordano, J. 1982: *Ethnicity and Family Therapy.* New York: Guilford.

McKinnon, L. & Miller, D. 1987: 'The new epistemology and the Milan approach: feminist and sociopolitical considerations.' *Journal of Marital & Family Therapy,* 13(2):139-155.

Maslow, A. 1970: *Motivation and Personality, 2nd ed.* New York: Harper & Row.

Maturana, H. & Varela, F. (eds) 1980: *Autopoesis and Cognition: The realisation of the living.* Boston: Reidel.

Maturana, H. & Varela, F. (eds) 1987: *The Tree of Knowledge.* Boston: Shambhala.

Ritterman, M. 1985: 'Symptoms, social justice, and personal freedom.' *Journal of Strategic & Systemic Therapy,* 4:48-63.

Waldegrave, C.T. 1986: 'Mono-cultural, mono-class, and so-called non-political family therapy.' *Australian & New Zealand Journal of Family Therapy,* 6(4):197-200.

Waldegrave, C.T. 1989: 'Weaving threads of meaning and distinguishing preferable patterns.' Plenary Papers, Australia & New Zealand Family Therapy Conference.

Waldegrave, C.T. & Coventry, R. 1987: *Poor New Zealand: An open letter on poverty.* Wellington: Platform.

Walters, M., Carter, B., Papp, P. & Silverstein, O. 1988: *The Invisible Webb.* New York: Guilford.

White, M. & Epston, D. 1989: *Literate Means to Therapeutic Ends.* Adelaide: Dulwich Centre Publications.

(All names of families mentioned in this paper have been changed.)

Colonisation and its effects[1]

In the nineteenth century, the British believed it was their destiny to expand and rule the Pacific region, dreaming of a British Empire of the South Pacific centering on New Zealand, In the 1850s Bishop Selwyn launched the Melanesian mission from New Zealand, which created spiritual claims to responsibility among the islands of the South West Pacific, among them Samoa. The Christian missionaries were the precursors of the colonising settlers, and it is from the first contact of indigenous people with the missionaries that the story of colonisation begins.

Contact with missionaries led to profound changes in traditional life. The culture, values and practices of the colonising nation become the dominant ones, those that the indigenous people should aspire to in every area of life – religious, economic, social. Success and acceptance in that dominant culture is measured by how closely people can conform to the values and lifestyle of the dominant culture. In the process, traditional values, practices and structures were devalued or destroyed. Even more destructive is the belief that it is only the colonising nation which is capable of making judgements about what is valuable or otherwise in the indigenous culture.

The missionaries altered the balance of life in Samoa, and this is particularly apparent in the redistribution of power between men and women. Because the Church was hierarchical, and its patriarchal missionaries contributed to the institutionalising of the oppression of women.

In 1918 New Zealand was granted a League of Nations mandate to govern Western Samoa. As in most colonial governments, economic policies were designed more for the benefit of New Zealand than Samoa. While Samoa gained independence in 1962, economic and personal links with New Zealand have remained close. The Samoan people have been treated as something of a human 'commodity' within the New Zealand economy, being brought into the country when unskilled labour is in demand, and expelled during times of heightened unemployment, with overstayers sometimes hunted ruthlessly. Upon migration to New Zealand, extended family and village structures broke down or were weakened, and the checks and balances which had always existed to regulate Samoan life and relationships were threatened.

For the Maori people, colonisation has led ultimately to their status as an alien in their own land. The Treaty of Waitangi has not been honoured, for the lands, forests, fisheries and chieftainship of the Maori people have not been protected. Statistics on all important social indicators show that the Maori people are seriously disadvantaged in gaining access to the resources of the country, and thus have never truly enjoyed the rights and privileges of British subjects as promised in the Treaty. Unemployment rates among Maori are more than double those of the non-Maori labour force, and there is evidence of widespread preference on the part of employers for European workers. The Maori and Pacific Island people are therefore the first to feel the effects of economic hardship and unemployment and are disproportionately represented in the poverty statistics, and hence victims of all the family and social upheaval and health problems which accompany poverty.

But even more significant is that the only criteria of success and worth are judged by white cultural standards, and Maoris have received powerful messages for decades that they do not measure up. Maori values and cultural practices and those of the Pakeha are often mutually exclusive. To succeed on Pakeha terms can mean having to abandon Maori values. Warihi Campbell gives this example: *In a Pakeha schoolroom the teacher may ask the children a question. A Pakeha child, knowing the answer, will keep it a secret and raise his hand. The teacher will praise him and he will earn status. A Maori child, if he knows the answer, will share it with his cousin and then be punished for cheating.*

It is not surprising therefore that after so many decades of colonisation, many Maori and Pacific Island people now perceive themselves as damaged and devalued. In recent years the Maori and Pacific Island people have become determined to throw off the effects of colonisation and embark on the painful process of resurrecting the values of their culture, and share its relevance and richness with the wider society.

Note

1. This piece was written by Carmel Tapping to provide some background material that is relevant to understanding the work of the Just Therapy Team.

The Treaty of Waitangi[1]

Central to an understanding of the cultural partnership which characterises The Family Centre is an appreciation of the terms of the Treaty of Waitangi. This Treaty was negotiated in 1840 between the British Crown and over 500 Maori Chiefs. The Preamble of the Treaty contains the rationale for the Treaty itself – a desire on the part of the British Crown to bring the white settlers under a formal system of law, to secure peace and good order, and to protect the Native Chiefs and Tribes of New Zealand and their rights and property.

The treaty itself contains three articles. In the first, the chiefs gave up governorship, (Kawanatanga), to the Queen of England. In the second, the Queen gives to the chiefs and 'all the people of New Zealand' the full chieftainship (Rangatiratanga) of their lands, villages and possessions ('taonga', everything that is held precious), with the restriction only that the Crown be given exclusive right of purchase of Maori lands should they be offered for sale. The Third Article imparts to the Maori people all the rights and privileges of British subjects.

On the surface then, the terms and conditions of the Treaty seem quite straightforward, providing little scope for ambiguity. However, it must he remembered that several forms of the Treaty exist. There is an English language version (which bears a total of only 30 signatures) and a Maori language version (signed by 482 of the 512 signatories), and translations of each.

Ambiguity is generated by the meanings some of the English terms held for the Maori people, and in the translation of these terms from one language to another.

In Article 1 of the English version, the Maori people cede 'sovereignty' to the Crown. However in the Maori version, this term is translated as 'kawanatanga', which means 'governorship', a term the Maori understood as describing a relationship of lesser status in a partnership. In effect, their belief was that only the shadow of the land would go to the Queen, the substance of the land remaining always with the Maori.

Further confusion arises from Article 2, in which the full, exclusive and undisturbed 'possession' of their lands is guaranteed to the Maori. The Maori version however contains the term 'rangatiratanga', which means 'leadership', 'chieftainship' or 'dominion'. But in addition, the Maori claim that if the British had intended the Maori to give up their sovereignty and chieftainship, then the word 'mana' (meaning influence, prestige or status) should have been used. Indeed, if 'mana' is what the Crown intended the Maori to surrender, then the Treaty would never have been signed, it being inconceivable that a Chief would surrender the mana of his people.

In any event, International Law requires that in any ambiguity in agreements between a colonising nation and the indigenous people, the condition of *contra proferentem* applies. This means that interpretations should be made against the party who drafts the agreement, and that further, the text written in the indigenous language must take precedence.

The Pakeha (Europeans) regarded the Treaty as a legal document, and over the decades have acted in relation to it as Europeans tend to do towards most legal documents – scrutinising it closely to determine how minimally they could comply to its conditions, and searching for 'loopholes' which would enable them to by-pass their duties and responsibilities under the Treaty. To the Maori however, the Treaty was a covenant, a testament, awesome in its sacredness and significance.

The Pakeha failure to honour the terms of the Treaty has resulted in the alienation of Maori from their lands, loss of self-determination, subjugation to a colonising power with its culture and values, and their relegation to second-class citizenship in their own land.

Recently the Ministerial Advisory Committee on a Maori perspective for the Department of Social Welfare advocated a policy of bicultural development (Puao-Te-Ata-Tu, or Day Break) as the appropriate direction for New Zealand. Among its recommendations were a commitment to attack all forms of cultural racism in New Zealand which result in the values and lifestyle of the dominant group being regarded as superior to those of other groups. The values, cultures and beliefs of the Maori people are to be incorporated in all policies, and there should be a sharing of power and authority over the use of resources, with these resources being allocated equitably.

It is this commitment to honouring the terms of the Treaty of Waitangi which guides The Family Centre in its day-to-day work with families and the larger social system, and in its staffing policies and structure. According to the Treaty, the relationship between Maori and Pakeha must be one of a just and equitable partnership, with the Maori people being recognised as the first people of the land of Aotearoa (New Zealand). They see their work with families, and their community development work in the larger community as based on concepts of social justice, accountable to their clients of Maori, Pacific Island or European cultures for meeting their needs in culturally appropriate ways. Alongside equity for the Maori people, the Centre is committed to justice for Pacific Island people in New Zealand. There is a recognition of the injustice they have suffered as a result of the colonisation of their lands by New Zealand.

Note

1. This piece was written by Carmel Tapping to provide some background material that is relevant to understanding the work of the Just Therapy Team.

2.

'Just Therapy' with families and communities

by

Charles Waldegrave

This chapter is the most recent description of 'Just Therapy'. While some passages within it are similar to those of the preceding chapter, it has been included here so as to convey the most up-to-date descriptions of this work. This chapter was originally published in G. Burford & J. Hudson (eds) 2000: *Family Group Conferencing: New directions in community centred child and family practice*. Hawthorne, New York: Aldine de Gruyter. Republished here with permission. Copyright remains with Aldine de Gruyter.

The rationale for a Just Therapy

'Just Therapy' was developed at The Family Centre in Wellington, New Zealand, to free both the practice and definition of therapy from its cultural, class, gender and modernist constraints (Waldegrave 1990; Waldegrave & Tamasese 1993). The domain of therapy was pushed outside the traditional clinical setting to communities. The critical contexts for knowledge and healing, though embracing the social sciences, were taken beyond its traditions to those that primarily define meaning for people. These critical contexts were (and are) culture, gender and socio-economic status.

Just therapy emerged in a reflective environment, where those who chose to respond to the needs of families and communities who sought help, did so in a manner that addressed the fundamental issues of our times that marginalise particular groups of people. These inequities have ensured the same groups of people continue to be those most in need of the health and welfare resources of our societies from one generation to another. The issues in New Zealand were not that different from those in other countries. They are centred primarily around cultural, gender and socio-economic marginalisation. The problem is that the therapeutic resources in most post-industrial societies were largely designed by middle-class intellectuals and practitioners. As such, they probably work well for like people, who have reasonable access to resources and place great stress on individual freedom. They have not been successful however, in substantially transforming the lives and lot of those whose cultures are marginalised, poor and, until recently, women. Those most in need of the health and welfare resources in these countries usually have access to fewer resources, and most frequently not on their own terms.

As this practice has not substantially changed since the development of modern social work, psychology and other applied social sciences, problems are passed on from one generation to another. Hosts of new middle-class intellectuals and practitioners are then paid to address the developing problems of the next generation of marginalised people.

The outcomes of this practice are quite inadequate. The inertia to change lies primarily in the powerful health and welfare structures that control massive budgets and efforts to define the social sciences as objective knowledge analogous to the physical sciences. Having taken this approach, other forms of knowledge and meaning creation, such as gender, cultural or class knowledge are marginalised to an inferior anecdotal status.

Just Therapy was developed to value these other forms of knowledge and help put a stop to the repeated inter-generational failure of applied social science to those most in need of the health and welfare resources, enabling transformative change to emerge out of those communities on their own terms.

The social, cultural, political and economic determinants

The Just Therapy approach is termed 'just' for two reasons. Firstly, 'just' refers to equity and justice. The work has grown up around the notion that many of the mental health and relationship problems people have are the consequences of power difference and injustice. There is certainly a substantial body of literature that associates low income households and inequality with physical and mental illhealth (Benzeval et al. 1995; Crampton & Howden-Chapman 1996; Kawachi & Kennedy 1997; Kawachi et al. 1997; National Health Committee 1998). We also know that cultural marginalisation is associated with illhealth (Durie 1994; Pomare et al. 1995; Bridgman 1997; Tamasese et al. 1997; Ministry of Maori Development 1998), and that abuse, in all its forms, has long term detrimental impacts on women and children (Walker 1978; Elvidge 1997; Luster & Small 1997; Calam et al. 1998; Gold et al. 1999).

Second, the Just Therapy approach attempts to identify the essence of therapeutic work. It is just (or simply) therapy, devoid of the commonly accepted excesses and limitations of some professional approaches and Western cultural bias. It is a demystifying approach, that enables a wider range of practitioners, including those with skills and community experience or cultural knowledge. The term 'just therapy' does not suggest a dilution of therapeutic knowledge and competence, but rather a distillation of therapeutic practices.

It was developed by a group of people at The Family Centre who wanted to push out the boundaries of therapeutic practice and apply a fresh critique. They also wanted to address the profound experiences of social pain that were not being adequately responded to by caseworkers, because of a narrower clinical focus. These were women and men, Maori, Samoan and European. Some were very highly educated and well qualified, others had barely finished the compulsory requirements of the New Zealand education system. Some were community development workers, some were family therapists; most were both.

There were a plurality of starting points and a plurality of knowledge and experience drawn upon:

1. The vast body of international social science knowledge.
2. No less important, the traditions of healing and the processes of healthy relationships in the three cultures: Maori, Samoan and Pakeha (European).
3. Gendered experiences as women and men.
4. A shared commitment to social justice.
5. And a belief in a universal spirituality that acknowledges the sacredness of people's stories, particularly in their exposure of pain. A view of spirituality that is essentially about relationships in all our cultures.

These five aspects were the pivotal points of collectivity in our early reflections, sharing, and debate.

Many families who came to The Family Centre located the onset of their problem with events that were external to the family – events like unemployment, bad housing, homelessness, racist, sexist or heterosexist experiences. These were extremely depressing ongoing experiences that eventually led parents and children into a state of stress, opening them to physical and mental illnesses. At first we endeavoured to treat symptoms as though they were the result of internal family dysfunction. After years of listening attentively to the stories of these people, however, we learned that for many of them, their problems were actually symptoms of poverty, unjust economic planning, of racism, sexism and heterosexism.

We learned that when people came depressed and in bad housing, and we treated their symptoms, we were simply making them feel a little better in their poverty. We were able to move them out of depression, but we then simply sent them back to the conditions that created the problems in the first place. Unintentionally, but nevertheless very effectively, we were adjusting people to poverty. Sadly, we realised that this is what most therapists and social workers do when working with poor or marginalised families. Furthermore, by implication we were encouraging in the families, the belief that they, rather than the unjust structures, were the authors of their problems and failures.

Liberating meaning

Psychology, social work and the other helping professions have been taught within a largely positivist and modernist framework. The claims to a superior professional body of knowledge often centre around the social science claims to notions of independence, neutrality, objectivity, and verifiability (Habermas 1971; Weiten 1995). Medical metaphors with notions of diagnosis and cure, and biological metaphors with a systemic focus are often used. The term *social science* is itself a metaphor modelled on the physical sciences. These all combine to create practitioners who search in varying degrees for objective diagnoses, objective causes, objective explanations and objective cures.

These processes have built a status of superiority for the social sciences over other forms of knowledge, such as gender, cultural and socio-economic knowledge. Over time this has created many problems, because the social sciences have grown up in environments that involve a range of assumptions.

Prior to the last quarter of the twentieth century, white men devised most of the theory and taught most of the practice. Books written in Western Europe or North America by such people were sold throughout the world. Thus the cultural assumptions of a healthy family for example, grew out of an environment where individual self-worth, choice and secularism in science were seen as primary values. They were then picked up and taught in cultures whose primary values centred around communal identity, genealogical ties and spirituality. To be professionally qualified, one had to adopt the dominant assumptions in training and practice. In Western Europe and North America, these assumptions are still dominant and African American, First Nations people and Asian cultures in Europe are expected to absorb them as part of their professional growth and development.

Many people however, remember the days when sexual and violent abuse was looked upon by psychologists, and other therapists, in clinical terms within the old medical, biological, and social science metaphors, characteristic of the more patriarchal assumptions of the times. Causes were sought, and symptoms were treated, but the abuse itself was often ignored or considered outside the clinical arena. Women politicised the issue however, and clarified the meaning they gave such events (Bograd 1984; Goldner 1985; Pilalis & Anderton 1986; McKinnon & Miller 1987; Kamsler 1990). Professionals could no longer act as they did. Abuse and the meanings we give it have changed our practice, our explanations, and the law. The tired old positivist metaphors were simply inadequate to the task. In fact, they contributed to a lot of unethical behaviour. It was the change of meaning to socio-political analysis that made the difference.

This was not discovered scientifically, it was the result of a political movement that created new awareness by drawing attention to the meanings given to these events. In a critical postmodern sense, the old practice was deconstructed and all its assumptions exposed. The chosen word 'abuse' floated a new meaning that highlighted women's experience and placed responsibility on the perpetrators. None of this emerged out of the so-called objectivity of psychology or the social sciences. A political movement identified the injustice and insisted that the practice be changed.

This is an example of the dubious assumptions in the development of social science knowledge. There are many others. The Just Therapy approach questions assumptions that lock people into disadvantage or injustice. In that same critical postmodern sense, the meaning behind assumptions are sought, where appropriate they are exposed and new meanings are created, which liberate and inspire resolution and hope.

Most psychological theories have been developed in Western Europe and white North America. In those cultures, as with Pakeha (European) New Zealand, individual self-worth is fundamentally important. Indeed, for practically all clinical psychological and psychotherapeutic theories, the primary goal of therapy is that of individual self-worth. That is because destiny, responsibility, legitimacy, and even human rights, are seen to be essentially individual concepts. Concepts of self, individual assertiveness and fulfilment are central to most of these therapies.

If you come from a communal or extended family culture however, questions of self-exposure and self-assertion are often confusing and even alienating. They crudely crash though the sensitivities in communally based and extended family cultures. Among individually based cultures, such questions can be quite appropriate. Outside these cultures, however, the questions are often experienced as intrusive and rude, because people in such cultures usually think of their identity in communal rather than individual terms. The questions can rupture co-operative sensitivities among people, and destroy the essential framework for meaning that should be drawn upon for healing.

Surely good social work and clinical practice should enhance people's sense of identity and belonging, but unfortunately the practices of applied social science have developed with Western cultural assumptions that so often render them ineffective with most non-white groups (Durie 1986; Pere 1988; Tamasese, Peteru & Waldegrave 1997; Waldegrave 1998). This explains why so many marginalised cultural groups fail to communicate with the social professions paid to help them.

Spirituality offers another important aspect that stands out. Social scientists often boast that their discipline is a secular science. They are suspicious of anything other worldly because they cannot measure or verify it. Families in non-western cultures frequently associate healing with spiritual practices and traditions. At The Family Centre, Maori and Pacific Island people when working with people from their culture often share dreams, prayers and numerous experiences that are important to the life of the family and the issues of health and wholeness. When violations are being talked about, there is often a need for spiritual rituals of protection. Those important aspects are considered sacred, and yet they are frequently disregarded by social workers and psychologists. As such the social or clinical work is perceived as being culturally unsafe for the client family.

The mainstream assumptions, which are usually considered by their proponents to be somehow more professional and objective, are deconstructed in these examples. Tragically, they illustrate a colonial mentality that ensures that the health and welfare resources never reach the marginalised cultural groups on their own terms. It is little wonder these communities continue their disadvantaged profiles.

Effective social work and clinical practice needs to be developed by people from their cultures. All cultures have people who have the confidence of their community and know the emphases and meanings that enable health and wellbeing. In a Just Therapy, resources are moved from ineffective mainstream outlets to cultural groups to develop their own paradigms that give dignity and add colour and variety to the field. Where these become effective and gain the support of their communities, they then need to be recognised as a new mainstream practice to be equally funded by government and private health and welfare funders. Furthermore, this process also enhances employment opportunities in communities that often have higher unemployment rates.

Just Therapy practice and Family Group Conferences

At the heart of the Family Group Conference (FGC) philosophy is the view that family relationships extend beyond the household or nuclear family unit. This was a major departure from mainstream theory and practice. It was an expression of Maori and Pacific understanding of the nature of family rather than the standard view that owed its origins to the British heritage of the majority of the citizenry. Genealogical connections, extended family concepts and communal processes were seen to offer greater safety for children than traditional mainstream approaches to placement, based on the success or failure of individual family units regardless of family ties. Furthermore, the new philosophy involved a shift in power from professional decision-making and placement with or without family support, to extended family decision-making with the support of the authorities. The two groups were now required to work together for the greater good of the children involved. For Maori and Pacific Island families, this naturally involved the extended family of aunties, uncles, grandparents, and so on. Although there have been some exceptions due to under-resourcing or family fragmentation, on the whole the young person or persons involved could be either placed and nurtured with close relatives or those relatives could support the immediate family to cater for the young person's needs.

This change of practice has certainly led to significant improvements, but the progress has been marred by a number of deficiencies in New Zealand, which relate to under-resourcing over time, the variation in skills of FGC co-ordinators, an inadequate understanding of the vastly differing definitions of self, and the tendency of the state officials to over-influence and constrain family processes. Despite these problems, the FGC has greatly improved family participation in decision-making in contrast to other areas of health and welfare services. Many young people (though unfortunately not all), who previously would have become lost in a distant institutional or foster system now remain a part of their extended families.

The FGC is a developed model for extended families to significantly contribute to decision-making when their children are at risk and have come to the notice of the authorities. As such, it offers a process, with a reasonably coherent theoretical underpinning, for families and authorities when working with young people at risk.

Just Therapy on the other hand offers a comprehensive approach to the range of problems families experience. Whereas the FGC has developed a particular process for one applied area of social work, Just Therapy has developed a coherent theory that provides the tools of reflection, analysis and action for all areas of applied social policy. The FGC, having drawn on Maori and Pacific cultural practice, has opened the way for more innovative and respectful ways for dealing with families in their specific area of operation. Just Therapy calls for this type of innovation in all spheres of applied social policy that will enable the field to recognise gender, cultural and socio-economic knowledge.

This involves a fundamental shift in power and meaning. At the heart of the Just Therapy approach is the recognition of women's knowledge and respect for their primary role in family life, recognition of the knowledge of marginalised cultures out of respect for their history and sense of belonging, and recognition of the knowledge of low income households out of respect for their daily struggle to survive. The Just Therapy approach encourages an action/reflection methodology (Freire 1972) whereby the cultural, gender and socio-economic contexts are addressed in every situation. We have learned that therapy was not something simply carried out with individuals, couples or families, but must also involve communities, cultures, societies and even countries.

With regard to culture, we are deeply committed to preserving the fundamental meanings, the modes of communication and ways of nurture of our client groups. This has enabled us to develop approaches that are congruent with their way of life. Maori staff work with Maori clients, Pacific staff with Pacific clients and Pakeha (European) with Pakeha people. Each cultural group has developed its own cultural approach to therapy and well-being, drawing deeply on their cultural traditions of healing and those aspects of the social sciences that have proved helpful.

This approach has had extraordinary impacts. Whereas Maori and Pacific families seldom voluntarily attended social work, therapeutic or counselling services, we were not able to handle the response from these families once they knew wise people from their communities would work with them using their own processes. It was not simply the fact that these people came from their communities, but that a modern approach to work with their people was carefully devised by them, taken to their elders, critiqued by elders and eventually launched with their blessing. This in turn, led to a process of accountability and partnership with the communities involved.

Before long we set up three cultural sections – Maori, Pacific Island and Pakeha (European) – each staffed with workers from those cultures. Each cultural section works independently and inter-dependently. From those sections we have developed a leadership management team that has one co-ordinator from each. This replaced the director position. Many staff members have been trained in the social sciences, but some have been employed simply because of their healing and nurturing skills which have been recognised by their cultural communities. Our partnership with these communities has often led to their putting forward, and our agreeing to, the person or persons they want to see fill a vacant position.

We have also developed processes of cultural accountability both within and beyond The Family Centre. Each cultural section, including the Pakeha (European) one, has its own group of elders with whom it consults at critical times. The constitution of the organisation was changed to ensure full representation of the three cultures on the Trust Board of The Family Centre. Staff members are closely involved in many of the community and organisational networks in their cultural groups, ensuring that they are continually in contact with current local and national issues that concern their people.

Within the Centre itself, we have developed accountability processes. These have become fairly well known through our publications (Tamasese & Waldegrave 1993; Tamasese et al. 1998) and workshops. Essentially, they state that all work that involves Maori or Pacific people in any way is referred to their cultural sections and is always accountable to them. The Pakeha (European) section organises its own affairs, but is accountable to the other two sections. Thus the Maori and Pacific Island sections carry out the role of guardians of cultural equity at The Family Centre. We often meet in cultural caucuses to work through an important issue separately, before discussing it together in the larger group.

These processes have been very important in developing a just integrity to our cultural work. They have been designed to ensure that the subtle modern processes of cultural dominance by one group, does not continue to colonise. In doing so, they also ensure that the cultural communities involved are able to develop their own processes and draw upon their cultural knowledge for healing and wholeness. In the process, more of their people have been employed, more educational forums have been led by them, more papers have been written by them, more organisations have been inspired to develop similar processes, and so on.

This has led to a rich diversity of practice at The Family Centre that has enriched discussion and ways of working. As Maori and Pacific groups have drawn upon the social sciences in aspects of their work, so the Pakeha (European) section have drawn upon innovative aspects of the Maori and Pacific work, such as the use metaphor in bringing about change and greater attention to notions of sacred events and processes in ordinary life.

These same principles have also been applied to our gender work. Using a feminist analysis to all our activities, we have endeavoured to address the issues of gender justice. This is particularly important in work with families where women are so primary, when addressing abuse and the ongoing issue of the feminisation of poverty, particularly for single parent, women-led families. We have developed similar notions of accountability in the gender arena as we have in the cultural arena.

All gender work, including the running of men's groups, is accountable to the women in the agency. When making significant decisions in this area, we often first break into gender caucuses before discussing as a large group. Similar to the cultural approach, the men in the agency are accountable to the women. The women have been appointed the guardians of gender equity at The Family Centre. Those who have been unjustly treated in the broader society, i.e. women and those from marginalised cultures, are considered to be the most informed about equity issues in these areas. In these ways, we endeavour to create a work environment that ensures we reflect the values we wish to pass on to our various client groups.

We have also endeavoured to address the socio-economic contexts of those we relate to by expanding our understanding of social and case work. That work has on occasions led us into a range of community work initiatives. These include helping set up an unemployed workers union in our area, a national housing advocacy group, separate Maori, Pacific Island and Pakeha (European) men for non-violence groups, a street kids project, a Kaumatua group (Maori elders) and a Samoan Stop Abuse program.

We also lead a range of social policy research projects that provide solid data on the sorts of issues our client base experiences. These include the New

Zealand Poverty Measurement Project along with two other collaborating organisations (Stephens et al. 1995; Waldegrave et al. 1996; Waldegrave et al. 1997), socio-economic determinants of health work, Maori housing and Maori and income projects and a Samoan mental health project. Thus, those who work with families also work in these other areas and are informed by the community and research work.

Some families we work with choose to participate in the community projects. Others simply know that we are as committed to the preventive work through community development projects, the research and advocacy, as we are to the casework. We no longer address the symptoms of poverty and racism for example, while ignoring the causes. We have developed a congruence between our casework and the rest of the work at the Centre. Each informs the other. For example, we can be much more helpful to families in housing need when we work on housing projects and carry out research that highlights the levels of deprivation. We have a hands-on knowledge of life beyond the clinical room which transforms both the conversations and processes of casework.

When working with families, we always try to honour the stories of survival of poor people, that most other professional groups refer to as failures. Some families are referred to us in incredibly derogatory ways as 'multi-problem families', for example. We often discover these people have suffered extreme disadvantage and developed many survival skills. Families who are forced to live in overcrowded houses for example, often live under extreme stress. There is nothing more basic to a family and family health than a house. We endeavour to untangle the malign threads of meaning and weave new patterns of resolution and hope. We commend such people for surviving the housing crisis with their family still intact. We recognise their ability to survive the crisis not of their making, but the failure of policy makers and planners, as courageous, committed and extraordinarily competent. We often add quite truthfully, that if our families had to go through what they have been through, we are not sure we would have had the same courage and found ourselves in the same circumstances. In doing so, we are recognising certain socio-economic realities and encouraging the recognition of powerful inner strengths.

Belonging, sacredness and liberation

We have learned to create our own metaphors that better reflect the warmth of our engagement with our community, than the cold social science ones. When describing case or therapeutic work, we often use the analogy of weaving. Although the symbolism of weaving is international, it is particularly appropriate in this context, because it evokes the activity of many women in the South Pacific Ocean. People come with problem-centred webs of meaning, and the task of the caseworker is to weave new threads of meaning and possibility that give new colour and new textures. The weaving should loosen the tight and rigid problem-centred pattern, enabling resolution and hope.

Another metaphor we often use is that of spirituality. By spirituality, we are not referring to christian institutionalism, but to something more akin to the sacredness of life or 'soul' as in soul music. For us the therapeutic conversation is a sacred encounter, because people come in great pain and share their story. The story is like a gift, a very personal offering given in great vulnerability. It has a spiritual quality. It is not a scientific pathology that requires removal, nor is it an ill-informed understanding of the story that requires correction. It is rather a person's articulation of events, and the meaning given to those events, which have become problematic. The therapist honours and respects the story, and then in return gives a reflection that offers alternative liberating meanings that inspire resolution and hope.

Finally, we have chosen three primary concepts that characterise our Just Therapy approach. When assessing the quality of our work, we measure it against the interrelationship of these three concepts. The first is *belonging*, which refers to the essence of identity, to who we are, our cultured and gendered histories, and our ancestry. The second is *sacredness,* which refers to the deepest respect for humanity, its qualities and the environment. The third is *liberation*, which refers to freedom, wholeness and justice. We are interested in the inter-dependence of these concepts, not one without another. Not all stories of belonging are liberating, for example, and some experiences of liberation are not sacred. We are interested in the harmony between all three concepts as an expression of Just Therapy.

References

Benzeval, M., Judge, K. & Whitehead, M. (eds) 1995: *Tackling Inequalities in Health: An agenda for action.* London: King's Fund.

Bograd, M. 1984: 'Family systems approach to wife battering: A feminist critique.' *American Journal of Orthopsychiatry*, 54 (4): 558-568.

Bridgman, G. 1997: 'Appendix 1, Mental health data presented to participants.' In Tamasese K., Peteru, C. & Waldegrave, C. 1997: *Ole Taeao Afua, The New Morning: A qualitative investigation into Samoan perspectives on mental health and culturally appropriate services.* Lower Hutt, Wellington: The Family Centre.

Calam, R., Horne, L., Glasgow, D. & Cox, A. 1998: 'Psychological disturbance and child sexual abuse: A follow-up study.' *Journal of Child Abuse and Neglect*, 22(9):901-913.

Crampton, P. & Howden-Chapman, P. (eds) 1996: *Socioeconomic Inequalities and Health.* Institute of Public Policy, Victoria: University of Wellington.

Durie, M. 1994: *Whaiora:Maori Health Development.* Auckland: Oxford University Press.

Durie, M. 1986: *Maori Health: Contemporary issues and responses,* Auckland: Mental Health Foundation of New Zealand.

Elvidge, P. 1997: *Health Consequences of Male Partner Violence Facts Sheets.* Health Promotion Unit: Auckland Health Care.

Freire, P. 1972: *Pedagogy of the Oppressed.* Harmondsworth: Penguin. 20th rev ed 1995, Continuum Publishing Group.

Giroux, H. 1983: *Theory and Resistance in Education: A pedagogy for the opposition.* London: Heinemann.

Gold, S., Lucenko, B., Elhai, J., Swingle, J. & Sellers, A. 1999: 'Comparison of psychological/psychiatric symptomatology of women and men sexually abused as children.' *Journal of Child Abuse and Neglect*, 23(7)683-692.

Goldner, V. 1985: 'Feminism and Family Therapy.' *Family Process*, 24: 31-47.

Habermas, J. 1971: *Knowledge and Human Interest,* trans. J Shapiro. Boston: Beacon Press.

Harré Hindmarsh, J. 1993: 'Alternative family therapy discourses: It is time to reflect (critically).' *Journal of Feminist Family Therapy,* 5(2):2-28.

Kamsler, A. 1990: 'Her-story in the making: Therapy with women who were sexually abused in childhood.' In White, C. & Durrant, M. (eds): *Ideas for Therapy with Sexual Abuse.* Adelaide: Dulwich Centre Publications.

Kawachi, I. & Kennedy, B. 1997: 'Health and social cohesion: Why care about income inequality?' *Brit Med J,* 314:1037-40.

Kiwachi, I., Kennedy, B., Lochner, K. & Prothrow-Stith 1997: 'Social capital, income inequality, and mortality.' *Am J Public Health,* 87:1491-8.

Luster, T. & Small, S. 1997: 'Sexual abuse history and problems in adolescence: Exploring the effects of moderating variables.' *Journal of Marriage and the Family*, 59:131-142.

McKinnon, L. & Miller, D. 1987: 'The new epistemology and the Milan approach: Feminist and socio-political considerations.' *Journal of Marital and Family Therapy*, 13(2):139-155.

Ministry of Maori Development, 1998: *Progress Towards Closing the gaps between Maori and non-Maori: A report to the Minister of Maori Affairs.* Wellington: Te Puni Kokiri.

National Health Committee, 1998: *The Social, Cultural and Economic Determinants of Health: Action to improve health.* Wellington: National Advisory Committee on Health and Disability.

Pere, R. 1988: 'Te wheke: Whaia te maramatanga me te aroha.' In Middleton, S. (ed): *Women in Education in Aotearoa.* Wellington: Allen Unwin/Port Nicholson Press.

Pilalis, J. & Anderton, J. 1986: 'Feminism and family therapy: A possible meeting point.' *Journal of Family Therapy*, 8(2):99-114.

Pomare, E., Keefe-Ormsby, V., Ormsby, C. et al. 1995: *Hauora: Maori standards of health. A study of the years 1970-1991.* Wellington: Te Ropu Rangahau Hauora a Eru Pomare.

Stephens, R., Waldegrave, C. & Frater, P. 1995: 'Measuring poverty in New Zealand.' *Social Policy Journal of New Zealand*, 5, December.

Tamasese, K. & Waldegrave, C. 1993: 'Cultural and gender accountability in the "just therapy" approach.' *The Journal of Feminist Family Therapy*, 5(2), Summer.
- Reprinted in *Dulwich Centre Newsletter*, 1994 Nos.2&3.

Tamasese, K., Peteru, C. & Waldegrave, C. 1997: *Ole Taeao Afua, The New Morning: A qualitative investigation into Samoan perspectives on mental health and culturally appropriate services.* Lower Hutt, Wellington: The Family Centre.

Tamasese, K., Waldegrave, C., Tuhaka, F. & Campbell, W. 1998: 'Furthering conversation about partnerships of accountability: Talking about issues of leadership, ethics and care.' *Dulwich Centre Journal*, No.4.

Waldegrave, C. 1990: 'Just therapy.' *Dulwich Centre Newsletter*, 1:5-46.

Waldegrave, C. & Tamasese, K. 1993: 'Some central ideas in the "just therapy" approach.' *Australian and New Zealand Journal of Family Therapy*, 14(1):1-8.
- Reprinted 1994 in Mumford, R. & Nash, M. (eds): *Social Work in Action.* Palmerston North: Dunmore Press.
- Reprinted 1994 in *Human Systems: The journal of systemic consultation and management*, 5(3&4).
- Reprinted 1994 in *The Family Journal* (The Official Journal of the International Association of Marriage and Family Counsellors), 2(2), April.

Waldegrave, C., Stuart, S. & Stephens, R. 1996: 'Participation in poverty research: Drawing on the knowledge of low income householders to establish an appropriate measure for monitoring social policy impacts.' *Social Policy Journal of New Zealand*, No.7, December.

Waldegrave, C., Frater, P. & Stephens, R. 1997: 'An overview of research on poverty in New Zealand.' *New Zealand Sociology*, 12(2), November.

Waldegrave, C. 1998: 'The challenges of culture to psychology and post modern thinking.' In McGoldrick, M. (ed): *Re-visioning Family Therapy: Race, Culture and Gender in Clinical Practice*. New York: Guilford Press.

Walker, L. 1978: 'Battered women and learned helplessness.' *Victimology*, 2(3&4):525-534.

Weiten, W. 1995: *Themes and Variations*, 3rd Ed. Pacific Grove, California: Brooks.

Partnerships across culture and gender

3.

Cultural and gender accountability in the 'just therapy' approach

by

Kiwi Tamasese

&

Charles Waldegrave

This paper was originally published in the *Journal of Feminist Family Therapy*, 5(2), 1993. Republished here with permission.

There is an increasing awareness these days of insensitivity and injustice in therapy experienced by women and cultural groups different from the dominant one. In the family therapy field, feminist writers and theoreticians (Goldner 1985, 1992; Harré Hindmarsh 1987; Kamsler 1990; Luepnitz 1988; McKinnon & Miller 1987; Walters, Carter, Papp & Silverstein 1988; among many others) have identified both the patriarchal determinants of family life and their infusion in therapy in modern Western societies.

To date, much less has been written concerning cultural bias in therapy (Boyd-Franklin 1989; Durie 1986; Gurnoe & Nelson 1989; McGoldrick, Pearce & Giordano 1982; Waldegrave 1986, 1990). There is, nevertheless, an emerging consciousness of the inadequacy of social science models that grow out of ideas from one culture being applied to another.

Social science theories, models and practices, for example, were largely formulated in one general cultural context – that of Western Europe and white North America. We have learned that social science is not a neutral gathering of information, as many have claimed. Rather, we have come to view it as one cultural way of describing events. When these descriptions are imposed on families of subjugated cultures, where understandings of behaviour and healing are quite different, the opposite of healing often occurs. This is because their places of belonging – their cultures – are displaced in the process.

Literature on these subjects identifies the biases in mainstream theory and practice, and offers alternative processes and personnel to overcome gender and cultural bias. By personnel, we refer to women therapists being more appropriate to address many of the problems women come with to therapy. Likewise, therapists of the same culture as the clients are much more likely to understand and facilitate the strengths of families of those cultures as they attend to the stresses that bring them into therapy.

The aspect that is not addressed in the writings on this subject, apart from our own (Waldegrave 1990), is the issue of 'accountability'. *How do workers, women and men and people of different cultures in an agency or institution, protect against gender and cultural bias in their work on a day-to-day basis? Furthermore, how do they do this in societies where sexist and racist assumptions are an integral part of the upbringing and way of life, as they are in most modern industrial states?*

It is surprising that so little has been written on this aspect around which so many organisations experience conflict. Most therapists have experienced the situation where a group that has been unjustly treated in society begins to raise subtle and not so subtle experiences of discrimination which they discern among their colleagues and in their workplace. When such discussions centre on issues of culture and gender, feelings can run very high.

In our experience, therapists, who are usually very concerned to facilitate resolution in the conflicts of others, tend to be very slow to address these issues among themselves. Instead, people on both sides of the conflict retire hurt, and are left to carry a mixture of feelings of fear, outrage and distrust. This does not inspire in the organisation an atmosphere of co-operation and respect. These are two of the values that are necessary for both a just institution and a just therapy.

Naming the injustice

When an individual or a group articulates concerns about gender or cultural bias within an organisation, relationships can quickly become precarious. The naming of this problem conflicts with the status quo, and feelings of comfort immediately dissipate, especially among therapists with whom one can expect to have acute sensitivity to the pain of others. The experience can be disturbing, upsetting, guilt-inducing, and polarising and generally creates disharmony.

This article is not written to address situations where outright hostility or total rejection of such claims occur. Our concern is with the liberal therapeutic environment where such claims are often acknowledged, but subtly avoided. In our experience three common outcomes of such naming strengthen the resistance to change. These we identify as 'paralysing', 'individualising' and 'patronising' responses.

Naming an injustice is an essential early step in the process of overcoming it. It usually highlights the issue, and relieves some tension in the person or group that considers they have been unjustly treated. Likewise, it often encourages a self-conscious reflection in the person or group that is considered to have acted unjustly. This too, is an essential part of any process of change.

Obstructions to this process occur when there is a recognition of some substance to the claim, but terrible fears about its implications. Men, in particular, though not exclusively, are susceptible to this in conversations on gender. So too are white people, women and men, in conversations on culture. They are often too nice to fight it; they just become paralysed.

Paralysis is a guilt response that takes in the criticism and deeply experiences the shame associated with it. The problem with it is that many people can't move beyond it. They note the complaint, agree with it, and offer sympathetic responses. Many people in this situation feel overwhelmed with the enormous process of changing the institution they work in, afraid of the bewildering implications for their own future and the possibility they might cause the same offence some time in the future. To avoid these risks and open conflict, they do nothing and feel impotent. Unfortunately, the passivity functions as a form of control because it further entrenches the status quo.

Individualising is a closely associated response when threatened with criticisms of cultural or gender oppression. 'Liberal' white people and 'sensitive' guys, somehow, separate themselves from their cultural and gender histories, and claim they can only be responsible for their personal behaviour. They then attempt to be individual paragons of cultural or gender equality.

The problem with this approach is that it cleverly sidesteps the institutional and collective reality of the problem of discrimination. It is the collective of men and the history of patriarchy which has created the environment that privileges the decisions and actions of men over women. No matter how committed to women a man may be, he may still continue to benefit at every level in a patriarchal society, at their expense.

Individualising the problem avoids both the sense of belonging and the responsibility to change the fundamental problem. I, a white person (one of the authors), was not alive when my ancestors and others colonised New Zealand. As a result of it, however, I have grown up with access to resources and other privileges denied to many Maori people. I now have the choice of working with my own to stop this collusion, or to continue benefiting from it. Individualising does not address this basic issue.

The *patronising* response is more crude, but no less common than the other two. It refers to people from the discriminating group who U-turn to such an extent that they become self-appointed spokespeople for the group their culture or gender oppresses. Men start speaking for women, and white people become the articulators for discriminated cultures. Not only is this sort of response quite inappropriate, it is likely to be inaccurate and resented.

Responsible partnerships between
the genders and the cultures

In the 'Just Therapy' approach, we have endeavoured to discover a way that responsibly addresses the institutional and individual modes of cultural and gender discrimination. The approach attempts to reverse the societal bias against women and the dominated cultural groups.

Cultural sections and gender caucuses

Within our overall collective at The Family Centre, the Maori and Pacific Island sections are self-determining. The Pakeha (white) section, because it is the dominant culture, runs its own affairs, but is accountable to the other two sections. Although all staff are committed to developed concepts of equality, unintentional impositions are still likely to occur because of our cultural histories. This accountability ensures an ongoing process of monitoring against intrusion into the processes of the groups that are dominated in the wider society.

Likewise, the women and the men caucus separately at times to address their own issues. As with the cultural work, we have found it helpful to agree to creative forms of accountability and monitoring that address our gendered histories and consequent biases. The women's work is self-determining. The men manage their affairs and responsibilities, but are accountable to the women. The point of such caucuses is to highlight the particular concerns of key groups so that their needs are not lost in a compromised partnership.

Cultural caucuses have now been institutionalised as cultural sections. With regard to gender, we have formalised groupings of men and groupings of women into separate caucuses. The women's caucus call the men's caucus to a meeting when an issue of injustice is felt in staff relationships, models or practice.

Issues are laid out, and a convergence of meanings is sought about the incidence. This may take one or several meetings depending on the complexity of the issues. Policy decisions emanate from these discussions. Meetings can also be called where a group wishes to put forward innovative ideas for discussion. We set clear boundaries to ensure the caucuses carry out their responsibilities. For those associated with injustice, the primary responsibility is to collectively transform attitudes, values, structures and forms of relationships that dominate. The responsibility of the subjugated groups is to identify their pain, recover their untold stories, and articulate their direction in relation to others who share the same pain.

Caucusing enables a collective of voices to speak as one. It is particularly helpful where a gender or cultural grouping has fewer numbers and lower status positions in an organisation. Their collective voice can be heard in a more equal manner. We value the voice of each individual in many discussions. On other occasions, it is important to hear the collective voice of women, of men, or of different cultural groups. Having met together previously, each caucus can share both their concerns and responsibilities. This sets up a different dynamic and focus in discussion.

Radicalising modes of accountability

The unique aspect of this approach is the reversal of usual modes of accountability. Because management and decision-making is commonly exercised primarily by men or white people, the patriarchal and racist assumptions in society simply permeate the therapeutic community. Our reversal consists of full recognition of dominated groups to be self-determining, and a requirement of the dominant groups to check out key aspects of their orientation and projects with the other groups.

This process has been very effective, because it enables a genuine monitoring of discriminatory behaviours and processes. In our view, the best judges of injustice are the groups that have been unjustly treated. Thus, the women are accorded the role of guardians of gender equity, and the Maori and Pacific Island sections the guardians of cultural equity at The Family Centre.

They have the right at any time to call the agency, or parts of it, to address equity issues. When they do, the agency is absolutely committed to seeking a solution that satisfies the guardians to whom the rest of the agency is accountable. This is not an authoritarian process. We endeavour to seek a consensus that we can practice with integrity, that satisfies those to whom we are accountable.

Sometimes an issue can be satisfactorily resolved in one meeting. On other occasions, where the issues require a lot of discussion and fundamental shifts in thinking, resolution may take a number of meetings over months. We persist until those to whom we are accountable consider their concerns have been adequately dealt with. The commitment not to give up has enhanced trust and facilitated creative solutions.

In practice, when the Maori or Pacific Island sections or the women have a grievance, we usually move through the following process:

1. *Institutional Space*
Time is set aside to hear the cause of concern. The group that considers they or their people have been unjustly treated, or an agency practice needs to be changed, are accorded uninterrupted space to tell their story. We refer to this as institutional space, because so many agencies do not set time aside for such a process and, if they do, they often don't allow uninterrupted space. Only after all the aggrieved people have articulated their concerns can discussion ensue, initially around points of clarification on both sides. This first step involves hearing the story, and the meanings the group is giving to events that have occurred.

2. *Converging of Meaning*
The group associated with the injustice is then committed to listen as openly as possible and authenticate the complaint in whichever aspects they can, with integrity, agree. This is not an empty-headed agreement. After clarification of any misunderstandings and points of fact, we usually discover substance in the concerns that have been brought forward.

Most white therapists and most male therapists, for example, would avow anti-racist and anti-sexist practices. The difficulty they have in practice is that they seldom experience what discriminated people experience. Furthermore, they are seldom in situations where they are required to respond to the issues raised by a caucus of colleagues with stories that are very different from their own. They arc usually aware of the stories of at least some discriminated people, however, and, if invited to authenticate a complaint, they usually can.

The authentication from the group associated with the injustice enables a converging of meaning between the two parties. Where this occurs authentically it is very painful, but anti-sexist and anti-racist learnings take root in an organisation. Furthermore, an analysis has taken place and the substantive issues have been agreed on, which enables some practice goals to be set towards resolution.

It is important to note that this process does not occur cheaply. We are not interested in 'politically-correct guilt' or 'white and male flagellation'. Our concern springs from the pain of our colleagues who feel we have failed them. We trust their pain and their ability to discern the significant obstacles, and they trust us to take them seriously and act honourably. The process is a vulnerable one for both sides.

3. Addressing Our Own

Having reached considerable agreement about the problem, and having shared the emotional pain of the hurt that has come between us, we begin to carve out a better future together. Sometimes the problems centre directly around our own actions. On other occasions they centre around sexist and racist practices that impinge on the agency from outside, which we could have done more to prevent.

Male therapists, for example, are often insensitive to the feelings of violation female therapists may experience when working with a family in which abuse has occurred. Likewise, a narrow clinical focus can completely overlook the constant strain and pressure therapists from dominated cultures experience, when working with their own people. The people they work with usually have so few of society's resources allocated to them. These experiences can raise broader contextual and social policy priorities for an organisation.

We endeavour to talk together with the same sensitivity and skill that we practice in our best therapy. Where we have directly hurt another, we apologise. When the pain is very deep we are sometimes 'unprofessional' enough to cry, just like the families that come to see us. After all, we tell them it is healing to cry, don't we?

We endeavour to discern the colonising and patriarchal influences around the problem, and try not to separate ourselves, our cultures, and our genders from our histories and current contexts. We deeply analyse the different meanings we give the same events, and try to understand and value marginalised meanings.

We then agree to new practices that deepen the respect and sensitivity among us. These new practices take on a collective, as well as an individual dimension.

Men in the agency, for example, are seen to be responsible, not just for themselves but for each other. The unenviable task of honing new sensitivities among men is not just left to women. Likewise, Pakeha (white) people are expected to develop responsible anti-racist perspectives among their own. These new strengths are not driven by reaction but by the deep commitment to honour each other.

Our agency often chooses to go a step further in this direction. We frequently take responsibility to address these issues in the wider therapeutic community, and even beyond that in society as a whole. It forms a central part of our writing, teaching, media work, research; and work in the community. As with the work in the agency, the dominating groups are seen to have a major role in developing cultural and gender sensitivities among their own.

4. *New Perspectives*

In our experience, this approach has inspired trust between the cultural groups and the genders. Because the agenda of the dominating group was jointly agreed to by the dominated groups, and because the latter have the powerful right to both monitor and call to account, a genuine partnership has the possibility to emerge. The quality of that partnership depends on the spirit in which it is carried out.

Though the processes are often painful, new relationships, new therapies, and a greater sense of wholeness is spawned. Probably most important of all, the therapeutic organisation begins to reflect and model the sorts of relationships we strive for among families. In our experience, most agencies fail to address the issues among themselves that they expect the families they see to work on.

We recognise that the creativity that has emanated from The Family Centre over the last decade has its origins in this process. The partnerships encourage us to consider different meanings and different processes. The Richness often gives birth to new ideas.

The trust that develops between groups, who in any other organisation nurse resentments, enables creative and equitable arrangements between the cultures and the genders. Stories and practices from groups that have been dominated become central to the life of the organisation. These include, for example, women's stories, cultural practices around greeting and food, processes during meetings, and spirituality in the broadest sense.

Over the years this process has helped us negotiate a path through many conflictual situations. The details of those discussions are obviously confidential as staff members have approached each other vulnerably. From a cultural perspective, we have addressed such issues as: the silence some cultures prefer to Western verbalisation; respect and time given to elders in some cultures that is comparable with the respect and time given to influential achievers and people of status in the white world; opportunities for expressions of spirituality in situations where Europeans often feel a little uncomfortable; and the setting aside of a greater proportion of the financial budget and other resources for hospitality and gifting which involves audit justification within the institution.

These discussions between caucuses require a lot of sensitivity. They are discussions that most institutions do not make time for, and so the dominating culture simply holds sway in that structure. People from dominated cultures usually politely co-operate with the status quo, and so the therapeutic institution mirrors the power difference that frequently occurs in the therapeutic relationship as well.

From a gender perspective, we have addressed such issues as respect for women workers' knowledge of the complexities, vulnerabilities, and potential dangers in family life. This has required men to stand aside and listen to quite different meanings given to events in family life from those which they were taught or experienced personally; changing every structure of our organisation to reflect gender equity and participation at all decision-making levels, from workshop presentations to the structure of our Trust Board; and the development of non-patriarchal policy guidelines as, for example, in work with men who abuse, that are overseen by the women in the agency. An example of this is outlined in another paper (Waldegrave 1990).

These examples are not an exhaustive list of the issues we have worked together on, to discover equitable partnerships. They simply indicate some areas that point to the types of discussions and dialogue we have become involved in. Interestingly, they do not only benefit the women and Maori and Samoan workers. Men, for example, have gained a greater sense of identity and co-operation as they have learned to recognise their vulnerability together. Pakeha (white) workers have also benefited significantly. One example is reflected in the new-found openness to the wisdom of their own elders. This has led to their direct help and input on specific projects.

Pain as a preferred meaning

The pain carried by many women and people from subjugated cultures who seek therapy from us, is not unfamiliar. We know its touch, its feel, its many, many faces. We link into it intuitively. For those of us from histories of colonisation and subjugation (one of the authors), the pain of loss is immense. As the Samoan novelist Albert Wendt has put it: *we are what we have lost* (Wendt 1991).

Consider this usual scenario: a country is colonised; her indigenous people made to live on the periphery and are enforced to ape the 'civilisation' of the dominant culture. They are then told that they will never make the grade anyway. Their histories, distorted/erased/dismissed, are left untold.

These are the faces of pain that we see daily as families seek therapy from us. This is also the pain that we as therapists from these cultures carry in so many institutions in which we work. We as women have a long history of being unnamed, cancelled, made extra, and having our contribution to humanity taken for granted. These are the faces of pain. It is also the pain of many women therapists.

'We are what we have lost.' Though the pain is immense, we, as women and peoples of subjugated cultures, can vouch for its potentialities for change. Such pain is not only directly inflicted, it can also be just as piercing through subtle passivity, non-action, and even silence.

Remember the instances when that pain became so immense that we refused to be allocated the peripheral spaces in conversations about models, theories and practices of our disciplines. Remember the times when that pain became so much that we refused to be lied to any more about our history. Remember our meticulous uncovering of story, the piecing together from the many fragments of memory. Remember the time when the pain of exclusion became so much that we stood up and claimed a central placing. Remember that!

The pain carried by women and peoples of subjugated cultures is real. It is a result of long histories of domination. The articulation of this pain illuminates behaviours, attitudes, values, and structures of domination. At a functional level, societies, disciplines, agencies, including family therapy agencies, cannot afford the non-hearing of this pain. Structures and disciplines of domination have caused the disruption and brokenness of many families – a brokenness our societies can ill-afford. Our only home for the human family – the Earth – has even been broken by structures, values, and apparatuses of domination.

At another level, the stories of pain of the subjugated, and the meanings they give to their stories, pose an interesting question. Do we see their stories and meanings equivalent to the stories and meaning of domination? We have referred to 'preferred meanings' (Waldegrave 1989) as those that are articulated by the people who have been unjustly treated.

For example, if we want to understand what has really happened in South Africa over the last century, we must listen to the meanings black people and their movements give to events, more so than to the stories in the white community. Because they experienced the pain of domination directly, they know exactly what they lost. This is usually underplayed in the white community. As such, the black story offers a preferred description of events. The same can be said of the story of a woman who has been abused, when compared with the story of the perpetrator.

This is not to say one group has the whole truth. Rather, it is to recognise hidden stories and the particular association of pain with truth. The stories of pain call from us an ethical stance, for: *Every human act has an ethical meaning because it is an act of constitution of the Human World* (Maturana & Varela 1988).

Accountability as vulnerability in trust

After hearing the cry of pain, one of the obstacles that block the way to creative change is the fear of role reversals. A common unspoken question is: 'Will they who have been unjustly treated exercise the same control and domination over us as we have over them?' 'Will they develop a blindness to our pain similar to our blindness to theirs?' These are legitimate fears, for all around us abound the culture, structures, attitudes and rituals of domination.

However, the cultural memories of the subjugated peoples hold vestiges of relationships other than the vertical arrangements of relationships that are characteristic in Western nations. These cultural memories are being recovered, for they often hold a differing value system of humility, respect, sacredness, reciprocity, and love that underpins new structures and processes of accountability.

For example, our analysis of pre-colonised Samoa revealed a covenant relationship *(feagaiga)* between brother and sister that had the capacity to equalise the relationships between women and men (Falenaoti 1992). The Western models do not always offer the liberative new structures that people are currently searching for. Accountability was institutionalised into The Family Centre as a result of our work with families of subjugated cultures and subsequently in our work in the area of gender. We made a commitment, in the first instance, that all our work with families of cultures, other than the dominant culture, would be accountable directly to the therapists of that culture. This was because the therapists of these cultures had the knowledge of their own people's stories, meanings, and rituals.

Our approach to accountability involves an act of humility. It requires a recognition that we don't have all the knowledge pieces to provide healing and wholeness to peoples of other cultures. Furthermore, a more critical and humble approach to the achievements of the social sciences, to date, is called for from us.

It follows from this that our models, theories, and practices in the Pacific Island and Maori sections are accountable to selected people of our communities. We hold meetings whereby we lay out our thinking and practice for our elders and co-workers to comment on.

Accountability, for us, is essentially an ethical process, a process that calls from all of us humility, respect, sacredness and love. It is required of all workers who are involved in healing, both those associated with domination and those associated with subjugation.

Cultural and gender accountability involves a dialogue between groups associated with opposite experiences. In dialogue we are mindful when we articulate, that we speak from positions of unequal power. We have created a structure that makes an open dialogue possible where hidden and exposed meanings are both addressed. It also involves a dialogue beyond the Centre, whereby workers in cultural sections go to selected members of their communities.

Accountability that fosters commitment to actions makes a difference to the lives of those who suffer. If it lies in the bedrock of values like humility, reciprocity, love, and sacredness, a mutual learning process can take place, for both those who call for accountability and those who respond. It becomes a mutual learning in vulnerability.

In essence, accountability is about the building of trust with the group with whom trust has been broken. Therefore, accountability in such a process is not about a simple reversal of roles in the hierarchical sense. It is an offering of vulnerability in trust to each other, so that the pain of injustice can be transformed.

The sequence of events

The development of this process occurred over a decade. It may be helpful to indicate some of the historical markers. In 1979, The Family Centre was set up as a family therapy agency. When we listened intently, we learned that many families who came to the agency associated the onset of their problems with issues outside the family system. They identified issues like housing, unemployment, racism, and sexism. It was the early 1980s and New Zealand was going through an economic recession.

The agency, after reflection, was moved to respond by opening up a community development wing to work specifically on these issues. This took place in 1982 alongside the therapeutic work. Reflections from this proved to be another turning point. During this period, the community work informed the development of family therapy, and the family therapy informed the community development work. The early signs of 'Just Therapy' began to emerge.

The marginalisation of peoples of cultures other than the dominant one took place even in organisations of the marginalised. Primarily, the peoples' senses of belonging were with their cultures. As a result, The Family Centre decided to move its community development work away from an issues base to a cultural base in 1986.

Three cultural sections were set up to address the issues in culturally appropriate ways, and to further develop their approaches to therapy. We removed the director position and, in its place, set up three cultural co-ordinators, one from each section, to head the agency. The Maori and Pacific Island cultural sections are self-determining. The Pakeha (European) section organises its own affairs, but is accountable to the other two sections. It was at this stage that we began to institutionalise accountability along the lines set out in this article.

We then developed gender caucuses. It became apparent in the gender area that a model of accountability needed to be put in place, given the disparity in the male/female positionings. In our caucuses the principle of collective voice is employed.

The institutionalising of gender and cultural equity is now formally reflected in our constitution of 1991. Our 10 person Trust Board is strongly represented by all three cultures, and women and men. Our constitution states: *The Family Centre is composed of a Maori Section, a Pacific Island Section, and a Pakeha Section. The sections are to be self-determining, co-operative, and are to share all resources equitably.*

The following statements comprise three of the seven objectives in our constitution:

- *Advocating for justice with particular reference to the prevention of discrimination against women and cultural groups, and the prevention of all forms of poverty.*
- *Providing cultural and gender-based services in family and community development work.*
- *Articulating and safeguarding the spiritual values of the cultural groups represented in The Family Centre.*

Finally, we do not consider our story as triumphal in any sense. We have walked a path which has many more challenges and obstacles ahead. It has been very painful and, on occasions, probably prompted some workers to move on. It has also been the source of great joy. We have no illusions that we have reached some Utopia of total gender and cultural equality, sensitivity, and understanding. It is precisely because we are becoming more sensitive to our own biases that we have set up these systems of accountability. There have been no models for us to go by. This approach is changing us, our relationships, and our ways of working. Hopefully, the next generation will find it easier because we and other groups have made a start.

References

Boyd-Franklin, N. 1989: *Black Families In Therapy: A multisystems approach.* New York: Guilford.

Durie, M.H. 1986: *Maori Health: Contemporary issues and responses.* Mental Health Foundation of New Zealand.

Falenaoti, M.T. 1992: *Sina e Saili.* In press.

Goldner, V. 1985: 'Feminism and family therapy.' *Family Process,* 24:31-47.

Goldner, V. 1992: 'Making room for both/and.' *The Family Therapy Networker*, 16:2.

Gurnoe, S. & Nelson, J. 1989: 'Two perspectives on working with American Indian families: A constructivist-systemic approach.' In Gonzales-Santin, E. (ed): *Collaboration: The key.* Arizona State University School of Social Work: Tempe.

Harré Hindmarsh, J. [formerly Pilalis, J.] 1987: 'Letting gender secrets out of the bag.' *Australian & New Zealand Journal of Family Therapy*, 8(4):205-211.

Kamsler, A. 1990: 'Her-story in the making: Therapy with women who were sexually abused in childhood.' In White, C. & Durrant, M. (eds): *Ideas for Therapy with Sexual Abuse.* Adelaide: Dulwich Centre Publications.

Luepnitz, D.A. 1988: *The Family Interpreted.* New York: Basic Books.

McGoldrick, M., Pearce, J.K. & Giordano, J. 1982: *Ethnicity and Family Therapy.* New York: Guilford.

McKinnon, L & Miller, D. 1987: 'The new epistemology and the Milan approach: Feminist and sociopolitical considerations.' *Journal of Marital & Family Therapy*, 13(2):139-155.

Maturana, H. & Varela, F. 1988: *The Tree of Knowledge.* New Science Library: Shambhala.

Waldegrave, C.T. 1986: 'Mono-cultural, mono-class, and so-called non-political family therapy.' *Australian & New Zealand Journal of Family Therapy*, 6(4): 197-200.

Waldegrave, C.T. 1989: 'Weaving threads of meaning and distinguishing preferable patterns.' Plenary papers, first Australia & New Zealand family therapy conference.

Waldegrave, C.T. 1990: 'Just Therapy.' *Dulwich Centre Newsletter*, 1:5-46.

Walters, M., Carter, B., Papp, P. & Silverstein, O. 1988: *The Invisible Web.* New York: Guilford.

Wendt, A. 1991: *Ola.* Penguin.

4.

Furthering conversation about partnerships of accountability:

Talking about issues of leadership, ethics and care

by

Kiwi Tamasese, Charles Waldegrave, Flora Tuhaka & Warihi Campbell

Publisher's note

Since the publication and widespread distribution of the article 'Cultural and gender accountability in the "just therapy" approach', by Kiwi Tamasese & Charles Waldegrave (1994), many different groups and individuals have been inspired by the possibilities of working in partnership across divisions of power and have tried to translate the accountability processes and structures of The Family Centre to their own contexts. Many of these attempts have been creative, positive and have led to generative actions in the broader world. Other attempts, however, although created from goodwill, have come across difficulties.

The following paper has been written in the hope of honouring the diversity of work that is currently being explored in relation to processes of accountability. It extends and builds upon the work that is documented in 'Cultural and gender accountability in the "just therapy" approach'. It particularly focuses upon the learnings of The Family Centre in relation to the role of leadership, ethics and care when trying to use caucusing as a way of furthering partnerships across divides of power and domination.

The process of creating this paper

The following paper has been created out of conversations that took place at The Family Centre in Wellington, New Zealand, between Warihi Campbell, Kiwi Tamasese, Flora Tuhaka and Charles Waldegrave. Cheryl White, Maggie Carey & David Denborough acted as interviewers. David then wrote up an initial draft which was completed in partnership with The Family Centre.

The processes of partnership and accountability within The Family Centre are concerned with finding ways in which people can come together across differences and relations of power to address issues of social action and justice in the broader society. Our partnerships are orientated towards the big picture. What goes on among us within the agency is an important foundation for the work we do in trying to play a part in transforming the society in which we live.

Over the last fifteen years within The Family Centre, which consists of Maori, Pacific Island and Pakeha (European) women and men workers, we have been committed to finding ways of working together that will provide a foundation for our work in our respective communities.

In order to work together we have had to grapple with the following questions:

How do workers, women and men and people of different cultures in an agency or institution, protect against gender and culture bias in their work on a day-to-day basis? Furthermore, how do they do this in societies where sexist and racist assumptions are an integral part of the upbringing and way of life, as they are in most modern industrial states? (Tamasese & Waldegrave 1994)

Developing processes of accountability

In response to these questions we have developed partnerships and processes of accountability which we described in an earlier paper (Tamasese & Waldegrave 1994):

Within our overall collective at The Family Centre, the Maori and Pacific Island sections are self-determining. The Pakeha (white section), because it is the dominant culture, runs its own affairs, but it is accountable to the other two sections. Although all staff are committed to developed concepts of equality, unintentional impositions are still likely to occur because of our cultural histories. This accountability ensures an ongoing process of monitoring against intrusion into the processes of the groups that are dominated in the wider society.

Likewise, the women and the men caucus separately at times to address their own issues. As with the cultural work, we have found it helpful to agree to creative forms of accountability and monitoring that address our gendered histories and consequent biases. The women's work is self-determining. The men manage their affairs and responsibilities, but are accountable to the women. The point of such caucuses is to highlight the particular concerns of key groups so that their needs are not lost in a compromised partnership.

Cultural caucuses have now been institutionalised as cultural sections. With regard to gender, we have formalised groupings of men and groupings of women into separate caucuses ... In our view, the best judges of injustice are the groups that have been unjustly treated. Thus, the women are accorded the role of guardians of gender equity, and the Maori and Pacific Island sections the guardians of cultural equity at The Family Centre. They have the right at any time to call the agency, or parts of it, to address equity issues. When they do, the agency is absolutely committed to seeking a solution that satisfies the guardians to whom the rest of the agency is accountable. This is not an authoritarian process. We endeavour to seek a consensus that we can practice with integrity, that satisfies those to whom we are accountable. (pp.58-59)

Our structures of accountability have been designed within an organisation committed to consensus – of which the dominant group is a part. The caucusing mechanism which is a part of the accountability process is not an authoritarian mechanism by which people associated with dominance or people of non-dominant groups take power or act over others with power. The structure of the process, through which issues are taken back into caucuses, is the shift in power that is required so that meaningful, dignified, respectful dialogue can take place. If the caucuses don't agree after a number of sessions then they go away and meet separately for a further amount of time. The caucuses then come together again. If still there is no consensus the groups go their separate ways for further time. This could occur over months. The process goes on until the group to whom the issue is accountable to is satisfied and until the dominant group has reached a place that they too can live with. This is an authentic dialogue. This is the meaning of partnership. It preserves the values of love, humility and respect.

A clarification of language

It seems important to clarify what we mean by the word accountability. The word 'accountability' and phrases such as: 'They've got to be accountable', 'You've got to be accountable to me', or 'Let's hold them accountable', are widely heard within New Right ideology and within management circles throughout western capitalist societies. The new market environment is increasingly requiring hierarchical, authoritarian accountability. The word 'accountability', for example, is currently being used to justify the de-funding of universities and social services.

As the New Right has had dominance of definition in the broader culture for some time now, it is all too easy for confusion to occur about our usage of the word 'accountability'. We must be vigilant to ensure that the language of the New Right, of hierarchy, authority, check-points, performance indicators and evaluation does not contaminate our attempts to carve out new territories of partnership. We are talking about ways of working that seek to give space to the marginalised, that seek to create the possibility of meaningful respectful dialogue across power differentials. We are trying to speak a language of partnership. Phrases such as: 'They've got to be accountable', are not born of a language of partnership – they are authoritarian statements. What we are seeking are partnerships of accountability which facilitate the responsibility of dominant groups to deconstruct their dominance.

Ongoing conscientisation

The caucusing process provides a mechanism whereby the marginalised can have a space within an agency and workplace. It is a mechanism which provides space for both caucuses to do their own work. We believe that a caucusing partnership structure can only work as long as it sits alongside a parallel process of conscientisation (Freire 1970) for both the dominant and marginalised groups. This occurs within the caucuses.

The primary responsibility for the day-to-day check and balance lies with the group that is associated with dominance. It is the dominant group's responsibility to continue to work on their consciousness around issues of power and all the biases associated with it. Members of the dominant group need to conscientise themselves and each other so that the responsibility for the call to stop certain sorts of behaviours, or certain discriminating practices or policy, is not left to the marginalised caucus. This is crucial. There must be a 'self-start' process in place because, once the process of caucusing becomes the only evaluative tool, it can become burdensome to the marginalised groups.

If the accountability mechanism becomes solely a check, an evaluative mechanism, there can be two profoundly negative consequences. Firstly, the responsibility begins to fall too heavily on the marginalised caucus to service the partnership. Secondly, the weight of this responsibility means that there is no room for meaningful partnership. The role of the marginalised group becomes one of increasing supervision and evaluation, while the dominant caucus becomes increasingly passive. The process becomes reactive and the possibility for a meaningful deconstruction of power is lost. The possibilities of standing together in new territories of partnership diminish. There is room only to relate within old hierarchical relations – even if sometimes these are temporarily reversed.

When the ongoing conscientisation process is working well, the relationship between the caucuses becomes less of a focus. The emphasis becomes one of self-determination for the marginalised group, and awareness and new action on the part of the dominating group. The primary work begins to happen within the caucuses, not between them, and the conversations that occur within the caucuses have positive effects not only within the agency but in the broader work that the agency is involved in.

Leadership

We have learned over the years that our caucuses require clear and consistent leadership. Dominant caucuses require leadership in order to prevent paralysis and individualising (see Tamasese & Waldegrave 1994, p.57). Marginalised caucuses require leadership to take care that stories of marginalisation do not build upon one another in ways that could spiral downwards.

Some groups advocate no leadership as a way of creating greater democracy. This is not the place from which we come. Although we too wish to see the end of patriarchal prototypes of leadership, we know that there are forms of leadership that do not replicate domination and that keep processes of accountability and caucusing safe. These forms of leadership encourage self-reflection that aids the deconstruction of power relations. This is the type of leadership we are calling people into.

Before processes of accountability and partnership are entered into, there needs to be a collective agreement in relation to leadership. This is particularly true for dominant groups as, all too often, if leadership is not structured and agreed upon, it will be contested, and all sorts of divisions can occur. This leaves the marginalised group more vulnerable to the process. It might be necessary for caucuses to meet first and work through what would need to happen to enable people/individuals to step into leadership around particular issues at particular times.

An invitation to partnership is not an invitation for dominant groups to abdicate their leadership or their responsibility for the process. Out of goodwill, dominant groups may step out of any form of leadership but in so doing unintentionally paralyse the process of change. It is the dominant group who is responsible for the deconstruction of their dominance. They should not give away their responsibility to play a meaningful part in consensus decision-making about the processes of partnership. Once again, before beginning a process of partnership, clarifying the common understandings about different responsibilities is crucial – especially within a workplace.

Leadership within the caucuses is very important. If people are going to use the caucusing idea they need to have leadership that is very clear about the purpose of each caucus in their particular context. If there are to be more than two caucuses then there must be enough leaders to facilitate them, and these leaders need to have worked together sufficiently so that there is one common orientation. Without clear and consistent leadership caucusing can become ineffective.

Institutional space

We believe it is important that workplaces put aside some institutional space and time for these issues. There needs to be some flexibility in management. The organisation needs to make a symbolic gesture of goodwill and demonstrate practical commitment to the issues.

Compromises will need to be worked through in a generous spirit. Configurations will work out differently in different contexts. At The Family Centre we work for as many hours a week that the issues need working on. It may be quite different in some workplaces. If people are working nine-to-five, for example, an organisation might allocate five or six hours over a period of two weeks. The staff may be invited to contribute some time of their own – perhaps matching hour for hour with the organisation. Workplaces need to work out what is sustainable and what are realistic goals and expectations.

Issues for the leadership of caucuses of marginalised groups

Caucuses of marginalised groups need leadership. People's pain needs to be collected, to be made sense of. A collective sense of purpose needs to be harnessed. Put simply, people need to be made to feel okay. The caucus is often the first safe place that people have found to expose their pain – it needs to be listened to. Ways forward also need to be found. It needs to be seen that people's stories are not solely a collection of pain, but contain obvious points of celebration and resistance.

There are various steps to this process:

Caucus as a space of building a clear collective voice
People will come to the caucus with different understandings of issues and of cultural marginalisation. In order for the partnership to work smoothly the caucus needs to get to a point of having consensus around any given issue.

Caucus as a space of healing for individual experiences of marginalisation
We know that people who come into caucuses will often have personal familial stories, or personal individual stories of hurt. Often they will not have had a safe space to talk about experiences of racism or sexism, so the caucus becomes the space where all of these experiences can be given voice. This can mean that the caucus is suddenly filled with one person after another connecting their painful stories to powerful common threads like colonisation. The caucus needs to be a place of healing these personal experiences.

When people enter a caucus with a great deal of personal pain from past experiences, they need a lot of support and space to heal in order to be able to safely take part in partnerships. A big question for marginalised caucuses is, therefore: are the people in the caucus in a place where it is right for them to participate in partnership? The caucus needs to be very clear about whether the group is in a position to engage in partnership.

Caucus as a space of knowledge-building

Throughout the process of developing a clear voice, the caucus is a place of cultural analysis and gender analysis. What also often takes place is a researching for liberative elements of cultural histories. This is very thorough research and is not to be underestimated. Within The Family Centre women's caucus there is often a sub-caucus of Maori women, of Samoan women and of Pakeha women. Each sub-caucus has conducted their research into their own stories. For instance, in the Samoan caucus it involved two women travelling to Samoa to look at the stories of Samoan womanhood. The Maori and Pakeha women's sub-caucuses conducted similarly significant research. Each sub-caucus found ways of representing what they had found, and the directions in which they wished to head.

Caucus as a space of negotiations of mutual interests

Within caucuses there is often a diversity of experiences. For example, within the women's caucus there are women from a variety of cultures. The caucus needs to be a space in which to negotiate mutual interests.

Through a process of separate exploration and research (as mentioned above), the Maori, Samoan and Pakeha sub-caucuses of the women's caucus have articulated each of their different interests. When the results of this search were shared between the sub-caucuses, mutual interests and specific interests were identified. If there were interests specific to any particular sub-caucus then a commitment was sought from the other two sub-caucuses to support this sub-caucus in their specific issue. For example, the Maori women are specifically interested in recovering their own stories, unearthing the liberative spaces for themselves, and the liberative spaces that are relevant to their relationships with their men and other cultures. The Pakeha women are similarly involved in unearthing liberative histories in relation to their womanhood, but they have a further responsibility to work with Pakeha men on the whole issue of cultural marginalisation and racism.

A similar process occurs when working in cultural caucuses to negotiate mutual interests/responsibilities between men and women of the same culture.

Caucus as a checkpoint for agency structure and policy

Caucuses often spend time discussing specific proposals that would advance awareness in the agency in relation to the group's experience. These proposals often involve issues like scholarships for people from marginalised groups to attend conferences/training, having some time from the institution to be a part of the minority people's caucus, etc. They are often cogent, small but significant.

Caucus as a checkpoint for therapeutic practice and underlying values
Caucuses may also be a place of innovation and thoughtfulness about current therapeutic work that is happening in the agency.

The leadership role in each of these areas is to facilitate the task at hand. It is also to care for and support all of those within the caucus, and to liaise with the leadership of the dominant caucus to ensure that when the groups meet together again that this is a generative process.

Issues for the leadership of dominant group caucuses

As mentioned earlier, one of the primary reasons for the caucusing process is for the dominant group to work with their own, to build understanding, and to take action. There needs to be an ongoing process of education by the dominant group with their own an ongoing process of deconstructing power. It can be difficult to maintain the energy within dominant groups to engage in this ongoing deconstruction, but we must be creative. If partnerships are going to work then we must find generative ways of working within dominant caucuses. What follows are a number of themes that we have found useful in relation to the sorts of conversations that occur in dominant caucuses.

Responsibility
The primary purpose of the dominating group is to take responsibility for injustice. Where the whole process can get off track is when personal individual issues are prioritised over collective responsibility. Inevitably people wish to talk about the hard times they have had (this seems especially true for men on issues of gender). People suddenly realise that the caucus is a place where they can get a bit of nurturing for themselves. There is a place for this. It's no good telling people just to be tough. Being trained into domination has its real effects, but the primary role of the caucus is one of responsibility. Leadership is really important to keep the caucus on track.

Team building

A crucial part of the process is creating connections between the members of the dominant group to build a collective identity. As teams of dominant people are traditionally based upon notions of superiority, how to team build around a collective identity that will not confirm dominance is a continual challenge.

Caring and support

These words characterise the conversations that occur within the caucus. There is space made for people to be able to speak of how they are coping with the issues and what they mean in their own lives. When we are addressing behaviours of dominance that we, others or institutions enact, it is so much easier to learn if someone is supporting us through the process and keeping an eye all the time on issues of responsibility.

Addressing the 'prime break'

The 'prime break' in gender caucuses is the break between women and men. It's not between fathers and sons or any of the other breaks that we may have experienced. In cultural caucus the 'prime break' is between the Pakeha (white) and Maori and Pakeha (white) and Samoan, etc. It's from this orientation the whole deconstruction takes place.

Self-consciousness

The deconstruction of the 'prime break' hopefully leads to increased self-consciousness. Explorations are made into the constraints which members of the caucus face in relation to their ability to be non-sexist, or non-racist. A self-consciousness begins to be built about our biases and also the lessons that have been learned.

Understandings of power and power difference

Issues of power are central to liberation, so a thorough exploration of understandings of power occurs within the caucus. Members' participation in acts of power and their real effects are deconstructed.

Collective responsibility

Finding ways of developing a sense of collective responsibility and collective care is perhaps the biggest challenge for dominant caucuses. Caucuses cannot work effectively if people within them wish to operate as individuals rather than as one of a collective. If people speak in discourses of their own individual rights as workers, or if people emphasise their own individual story and experience over the experiences of the marginalised group, it can make the process difficult. Building a sense of collective identity and responsibility seems especially difficult for white people. Within men's groups in which there are men of different cultures present it is easier. But within white caucuses individualism runs deep. What often really helps is that in partnership the dominant group has the models of the other cultural caucuses to learn from – especially in relation to building consensus. Nevertheless, building a sense of collective responsibility can take time.

Tracing liberative elements

Within dominant caucuses we have needed to explore and bring to life liberative elements from our histories that show other ways forward. Within men's caucuses we have searched for elements within the history of manhood that offer different possibilities than those offered by current dominant stories of masculinity. Men of different cultures explore different stories from their own cultural traditions – this is true also for white men. Men also endeavour to unearth liberative stories within their own family histories. Trying to find the contradictions to the stereotypes of masculinity within our own histories and traditions is an important part of the caucusing process.

To be able to constrain and extend one another

Gradually members of dominant caucuses begin to take responsibility for each other. Within the context of collective care, members of the caucus begin to gently interrupt oppressive behaviours in each other before the marginalised group have to. A collective pride begins to grow in relation to this. At the same time, seeing the caucus take responsibility for each other gives the non-dominant group the greatest confidence. If a member of the dominant group can pre-empt the actions of other members then this provides much more safety.

Honouring the other

It's important that the dominant group begins to honour the concerns of the non-dominant group. Over time this involves pre-empting issues that may come up and making changes so that the everyday concerns of the non-dominant group become a part of the institutional life of the workplace. For instance, for Maori and Pacific Island peoples elders are very significant. Providing time to welcome elders and acknowledge them within the workplace is an important aspect of the running of The Family Centre.

Making the caucus livable
Within the dominant caucus we have found it important to make the process liveable and sustainable. Events that lighten the process, like going out to dinner together, can play a significant part in ensuring that the process is not always associated with addressing painful issues.

Providing care for the group
The leadership needs to facilitate a process so that the group begins to take care of each other. Members of the dominant group need encouragement because they are starting something that is new and challenging for them. It is up to members of the dominant group to acknowledge and encourage each other so that they do not have to look to members of the marginalised group to provide it.

Values

The work of the caucuses, the partnerships within the agency, and our work in the broader society, are based upon carefully constructed values.

Accountability that fosters commitment to actions makes a difference to the lives of those who suffer. If it lies in the bedrock of values like humility, reciprocity, love, and sacredness, a mutual learning can take place, for both those who call for accountability and those who respond. It becomes a mutual learning in vulnerability. (Tamasese & Waldegrave 1994, p.66)

The values of humility, sacredness, respect, justice and love, trust and co-operation are absolutely central to our processes of accountability. Some of these values derive from our particular cultural context. For example, reciprocity is a significant value in Maori and Samoan culture which does not really have the same significance in Pakeha (white) culture. All three cultural caucuses have met and worked to establish what are the values that we wish to underpin and sustain our ways of working in partnership together. There has been a process of naming these values and building upon them. The words that we use now have been carefully chosen as they resonate with our particular histories. In a different context there would be different words and values.

It seems crucial that, prior to people entering into processes of partnership, they must agree to the bedrock of values on which their partnership will be based. Prior to initiating any processes of accountability it would be very important to invite the caucuses to consider a number of questions about the values that will underpin the partnerships:

* What are the values in their own culture/histories that will enable them to walk into partnership?

* What are the key values in their own culture/histories that will sustain this partnership, and that will hold the process together?

* What are the key values in their own culture/histories that will enable them to respect their partners in this partnership?

Both the dominant and marginalised groups will need to agree to these values before the process begins.

Creating new territories of partnership

What has also been extremely significant in our quest for partnership (and yet rarely focused on by others) has been the search for grounding our partnerships in history. We have always believed that this work is primarily concerned with ethics and history. That's where we link in with the narrative tradition. We believe that narratives need to go back into history (or forward into history from a Maori perspective). We need to look at the ethics and liberative narratives within our people's histories. Within all our people's histories there are non-liberative and liberative stories, traditions and practices. We are being selective about our histories. We are looking for the liberative practices and building upon these – building from strength to strength.

In particular, we have been determined to find histories of ways of relating that exist in territories beyond hierarchical arrangements. These histories are the foundations upon which we wish to build our partnerships.

... the cultural memories of the subjugated peoples hold vestiges of relationships other than the vertical arrangements of relationships that are characteristic in Western nations. These cultural memories are being recovered, for they often hold a differing value system of humility, respect, sacredness, reciprocity, and love, that underpins new structures and processes of accountability ... (Tamasese & Waldegrave 1994, p.65)

Throughout western cultures vertical arrangements of relationships and hierarchy are so common that within explorations of partnership and power there is always the potential to replicate these vertical arrangements, or to reverse them. All around us abound the culture, structures, attitudes and rituals of domination. Our quest has been to recover histories of different ways of relating:

For example, our analysis of pre-colonised Samoa revealed a covenant relationship (feagaiga) between brother and sister that had the capacity to equalise the relationships between women and men (Falenaoti 1992). (Tamasese & Waldegrave 1994, p.65)

This covenant has at times held our partnerships together, as Kiwi describes:

Even if we are in some way enraged with the action of the men's caucus, what is foremost at the end of the day is 'they are our brothers'. We recognise that pushing them into the river equals pushing us in as well.

For any partnership that is seeking to do things differently, that is seeking to step into new territories, there will need to be foundations. In different contexts people will do this differently. Within individualistic cultures the challenge to unearth/create liberative structures that do not simply replicate or reverse hierarchical ways of relating is a profound one. Faith and cultural traditions may be places to start, so too may be the histories of alternative social movements.

Speaking from a different place

Not only have we had to find alternative foundations for the partnerships, we have also had to find spaces from which to speak to each other which are outside traditional oppressor-oppressed relations, as Kiwi describes:

As women it has been important to name our oppression clearly, but stepping into a conversation with the men with dignity and with honour has required more than this. We have had to move to a space that is other than being 'the oppressed'. We have had to name oppressive acts, and to speak clearly about how these acts must stop, but equally importantly we have had to say: 'We are not here to meet you as the oppressed, we are speaking to you as co-partners. We are in this together. This is an invitation. If you would like us all to be working together, this is how it could work.' This is no longer speaking from a position of powerlessness. It is speaking from a position of empowerment. It is important that we caucus as a group until we can get to this point. It is a strong, dignified place. It is not stepping into acts of power over the dominant group. It is a new territory that we are stepping into. It takes the dominant group into a different space too. It has meant that when we come back from our caucuses we speak differently – with pride and a power that is not born of domination.

Developing partnerships of accountability around issues of sexual identity

In some workplaces these ideas of caucusing have been applied in relation to differences of sexual identity. Caucuses have been established to work on issues related to sexual identity and heterosexual dominance. This is not an area of caucusing which we have written about. The process of caucusing can have different meanings and implications in this area. Dilemmas can be raised when lesbian, gay, bisexual or transgender people who have chosen not to publicly identify themselves are invited into caucuses. Caucusing could unintentionally force them either to declare themselves or alternatively place them in a group with whom they are quite uncomfortable. Processes should be developed that address this issue. How to acknowledge the similarities and differences in experience of gay, lesbian, bisexual and transgender people is also an important consideration. Developing responses to these and other relevant issues would take care and thoughtful leadership. This model may require some adaptation to those circumstances.

Keeping the process positive

There is enormous pressure on all those involved in the process of partnership due to the seriousness of the issues. Acknowledging this brings a gentleness to the conversations. Within these partnerships, the steps taken by both groups are recognised and acknowledged – by both groups. Even though what may amount to the dominant group as significant might be only a few yards of movement to the marginalised group, it is recognised. The dominant group then recognises this generosity, and a positive cycle is developed.

When trying to address and talk about and work together on issues of power and oppression, it is very important that caring processes infuse the partnership accountability structures. This occurs both within separate caucuses, but also in the process of the caucuses coming together again.

If the non-dominant group is going to express their pain or hurt to the dominant group then this is handled extremely carefully and with great care. Often it is pre-empted with considerable gentle preparation: 'We've got some things that we need to share with you. They are not going to be easy to receive but they are going to be very painful to tell. These are things that really need time for reflection. We'd really like to hear what you think but we don't need any response today.' Such careful preparation creates a sacred place. It reduces the possibilities for defensiveness. It is then the responsibility of the dominant group to go away and care for each other through the process of taking responsibility for what has occurred and to find ways of taking action – both within the agency and beyond.

Taking care of trust

In essence, accountability is about the building of trust with the group with whom trust has been broken ... It is an offering of vulnerability in trust to each other, so that the pain of injustice can be transformed.
(Tamasese & Waldegrave 1994, p.66)

Trust is what makes this process work. Members of the marginalised culture or gender are in some ways learning to trust again through these processes. When trust is broken, it can bring great sorrow to the members of the marginalised group. Can we develop protective mechanisms so that marginalised cultures and genders are not left so vulnerable to situations when misunderstandings occur?

If there is a deliberate violation of a prior understanding and trust is broken then it is inevitable that significant injury will occur. However, what is more common within partnerships is that members of the dominant group inadvertently enact domination, and it is this that threatens the trust of the partnership.

Are there ways of protecting the trust that is crucial to the process of partnership?

Realism rather than romanticism

Sometimes breaks in partnerships may not have occurred if the partnership had been more realistic and open about what could have been achieved. When we are coming from different cultural thought constructions it is inevitable that there will at times be unintended difficulties. If members of dominant groups were able to be realistic in naming what they can deliver and what they can't deliver, perhaps people in the marginalised group may be more prepared for mistakes. However, this is a complicated area. How can ways be found to pre-empt inevitable misunderstandings that do not abdicate responsibility of the dominant group, nor deny the experience of members of marginalised groups, and do not detract from the urgency and commitment to challenge domination?

When entering into partnerships, it can be very easy to tap into visionary, utopian ideals. These ideals then energise possibilities. After two or three really good experiences these ideals and expectations are initially confirmed. When a misunderstanding then takes place the shock can be extreme.

How can members of dominant groups protect against hypocrisy by being clear about what is possible and what is not? How can it be ensured that the process does not become romanticised? How can members of marginalised groups take real care with their trust? A part of this care may involve finding ways back to the big picture.

Developing partnerships of accountability in different contexts

The structures we have developed are in a context of a small agency in which people are working in long-term committed relationships. We have never suggested that our ways of working can be easily translated into different contexts. It is clear that processes of accountability will not work in situations where any party does not want to, or does not feel safe. No marginalised group should be expected to go into partnership, and no partnership should be entered into without first both groups doing preliminary work to ensure that there is sufficient commitment, common ground and agreement to honour and sustain the partnership.

Some common difficulties that seem to be occurring as people try to instigate partnership/accountability processes in their own contexts include:

Leadership

A variety of common problems can be summed up under the heading of leadership. Some of the areas in which leadership problems have occurred include: a lack of importance being placed on the role of leadership within caucuses; division between leaders of the different caucuses; caucuses being established with no organised leadership at all and no mechanisms by which the leaders of each caucus will bring the groups back together again. Without good leadership it is possible for caucuses to escalate in the direction of despair and pain, and for the process to become divisive when the opposite is intended.

Caucusing as healing in itself

At times there seems to have been a belief that all a group needs to do in order to address an issue of injustice between them is to caucus. Somehow the act of caucusing in and of itself is seen as liberating, and that when the caucuses come back together again there is faith that relationships will somehow be enhanced. Unfortunately, however, where caucusing has occurred outside of ongoing partnerships, people have at times come back together in increased distress and the process has been divisive rather than enhancing relationships.

Maintaining a focus

If the initial caucuses are painful and divisive, attending to this distress can become the entire focus of energy. Ongoing accountability processes can become a focus in themselves, rather than as a facilitative structure to enable partnerships to work together on broader issues of injustice in the wider world.

Institutional power

At times, caucusing has occurred within workplaces or training courses with little regard given to the complexities of institutional power relations. Supervisors, management personnel or tutors/teachers have become members of a marginalised caucus while students, employees, supervisees have become members of the dominant caucus. Situations like this require great care.

Transient workers

Within The Family Centre, people within the caucusing process are those who have long-term commitment to each other and the workplace. Involving people within caucusing who will only be around for the short-term, such as students or visitors, may be complicated.

Practical constraints

Practical constraints have also created difficulties. The size of caucuses when accountability processes have been used within conferences and/or large workshops have greatly limited possibilities, as have time constraints. Attempting to use caucusing in time-limited contexts with large numbers of people can be problematic.

Focusing on the big picture

Throughout the processes of partnership we have had to find ways to stay focused on the big picture and not get caught up in minute differences or conflict. This is not always easy, however, and of course who determines what is a small issue and what is a big issue can be highly contentious.

As therapists, we bring to partnerships a deep sensitivity to shifts of power no matter how small they are. Whether they occur in conversation, in the kitchen, in the workplace, or in caucuses, our work within family therapy sensitises us to minute power shifts. This keen sensitivity to minute relations of power can complicate our work in accountability. Any small shift of power that occurs gets noticed and invites a comment. Our internal focus in family therapy orientates us to these small power shifts. What can then occur is that if we notice power shift A we might link it to power shift B. It is easy to make a jump of logic to link power shift B to power shift C. Suddenly a small shift in power is linked in our hearts to an act of gross oppression and a sense of outrage and injustice can escalate.

Remaining focused on the big picture is important. Our accountability processes are the foundation for the work we do in our respective communities. Our partnerships within the agency remain continually orientated to the work we do in the broader society. A common commitment to big picture change, and working together in relation to bringing about this change, generates trust. It is a trust that is based on collective action.

Conclusion

Within this paper we have tried to clarify some of the foundations upon which our partnerships of accountability are built. We have also tried to describe some of the recent points of growth. We have spoken of leadership, ethics and care, and we have evoked the liberative histories upon which we base our work. We have emphasised how important the initial processes of negotiating partnership relationships are, the importance of understanding power differences and deconstruction, and how consensual rather than authoritarian processes need to be primary. We hope that the more detailed explanations which we have provided here will prove helpful to others in their own endeavours to create meaningful partnerships.

These issues remain very complex. It took generations to build up the divisions, injustices and relations of power which we are trying to address. It will take some generations to overcome them. What we can do is make a start.

References

Freire, P., 1970: *Pedagogy of the Oppressed.* New York: Continuum.

Tamasese, K. & Waldegrave, C. 1994: 'Cultural and gender accountability in the "just therapy" approach.' *Dulwich Centre Newsletter,* Nos.2&3.

Publishers' acknowledgements

Dulwich Centre Publications would like to acknowledge the helpful feedback we received from Sue Hetzel, Zoy Kazan and Chris Behan.

Culturally appropriate therapy

5.

Therapy
as metaphorical
reflection

an interview with

Charles Waldegrave

This interview was conducted by David
Denborough, the staff writer of Dulwich
Centre Publications.

Elsewhere you have written and spoken about how the principles of belonging, sacredness and liberation inform all the work that you do at The Family Centre (Campbell, Tamasese & Waldegrave 2000). Could you possibly speak about how these principles influence the metaphors you are interested in bringing forth in your conversations with families?

Charles: The principles of belonging, sacredness and liberation influence all the work that we do. They shape the metaphors we evoke in conversations but also the directions of the organisation and everything in between. They guide our explorations. Let me just say a few words about these principles. By *sacredness* we are referring to our responsibility to uphold the sacredness of life and relationships. By *liberation* we are referring to the process of enabling people to create a destiny of their choosing, which is not only an individual matter but also often associated with a destiny for one's people or community. And by *belonging* we are emphasising that we believe that our health as people is directly linked to our sense of belonging – to land, people and culture.

The ways in which these principles work in practice are quite complex. For instance, although some have misunderstood our work in this regard, we do not simply privilege culture regardless of other relations of power. We have always talked about focusing on the liberative traditions within cultures. Kiwi Tamasese has used the metaphor of archaeology to evoke the idea of exploring the histories of our various cultures to find the liberative elements held within them. By the way, this is just as true for white European cultures as it is for other cultures. Around issues of gender for example, these explorations are informed by the question: 'When were the times in our cultural histories when women and men related in different ways?' Other explorations might be around the question: 'What are the stories of belonging in our cultures that talk about the special place of children and our responsibilities to them?' When families consult with us their lives are complex. We use the principles of belonging, sacredness and liberation to guide us in our conversations.

Can you speak a bit about what you are hoping to occur in these conversations?

Charles: The events that families experience occur in the physical world, and families then create meaning about these events. If a family has turned to therapy, generally speaking those meanings have become problematic in some way. So, in our therapeutic conversations, what we're wanting to do is to try to create the possibility for alternative meanings.

When we consult with a family the first step is to listen to the stories of the family. We do very little educational work, and the therapist's role for the vast majority of the interview is primarily to listen rather than to intervene.

While the interviewing therapist has been with the family, another therapist is often behind a one-way mirror. After listening to the conversation between the therapist and the family, the two therapists create a metaphorical reflection. This metaphorical reflection is then offered back to the family. We read it out twice as this creates a sense of ritual and acknowledges the significance of the family's stories.

Can you say more about these metaphorical reflections?

Charles: What we try to do with this reflection is firstly to acknowledge any thresholds that have been crossed. If violence has occurred for example, or any act of injustice has taken place, we underline this in some appropriate way. Then the purpose of the metaphorical reflection is to highlight and affirm the qualities about the family that have been articulated in the stories they have told, or are implicit in the stories that have been told. We are seeking contradictions to the dominant problematic story. We are seeking alternative meanings that could assist the family to break from the problems they are struggling with.

Within these reflections we float the alternative meaning on a metaphor. The beauty of metaphor is that there is room for people to make it their own, to interpret it in their own way, to actively make further meaning with it. The use of metaphor can free up what may have become very fixed views within a family. We find that this process of metaphorical reflection generates new possibilities, as long as we've really listened very carefully to people and have reflected something authentic back. By authentic I mean that our reflection must resonate with the experience of all the family members. It must resonate with their individual perspectives, and also their cultural context. This is not simply about creating a metaphor out of nowhere. I think a lot of metaphorical talk can be very empty if it is seen as simply a 'technique' to apply. Offering metaphoric reflections that resonate with family members involves more than technique. It involves an understanding of context, of history, of language and of culture. When done well, it can be quite stunning and experienced by the family as 'newsworthy', to use one of Michael White's terms.

Where do most of the metaphors you evoke in therapy derive from?

Charles: Most of our metaphors are lifted from the words spoken by the family and family members. Somewhere along the line, families generally speak with metaphors. Sometimes these metaphors are quite violent metaphors, however, and we choose not to build upon these (we may mention them to expose their danger, but we wouldn't use them to float deliberative meaning). And sometimes in a conversation with a family they might not use a metaphor that we feel we can build upon. In these instances we have to create one.

In situations where we are trying to craft an appropriate metaphor this requires great care. We always try to think of the three principles – sacredness, belonging and liberation – in this process. We try to think through the cultural context of the family, their sense of belonging, and any gendered issues that may be relevant. We take our cues from the words spoken by the family. The family will have offered us a great deal of information about what sort of metaphor would be likely to resonate for them. With Maori, Pacific and Pakeha (European) families, workers from these cultures develop the appropriate metaphors. In situations where we are working across culture we ensure that we have cultural advisors who can assist us in this process. We take sufficient time to create a metaphor which we hope will evoke a profound sense of belonging, sacredness and liberation.

Could you speak a little about how you came to be using metaphors in your work in this way?

Charles: I guess the person who's taught me more about metaphor than anyone else is Warihi Campbell. Warihi thinks in metaphors. I know that white therapists have written about the use of metaphor in therapy for many years, but for me personally I never took it particularly seriously until I recognised how characteristic metaphorical speech is within Maori and Pacific people. In order to understand what people were saying I had to learn to understand the use of metaphor. Obviously white people have been evoking metaphors from the beginning of our language, but for me I learnt about the significance of metaphor by being closer to Maori and Pacific Island people. It wasn't that they were teaching me, it was just that they speak in metaphors all the time. For instance, when we did the research into Samoan mental health and I read the transcripts of the conversations of the elder women, they spoke in metaphor, the meaning of which was quite incomprehensible to me. I had to ask Kiwi to explain it. I may have been living with metaphor for a long time but I just could not understand, while Kiwi, being Samoan could follow the meanings easily.

Coming back to Warihi though, let me offer an example of the ways in which he uses metaphor in his work with families. I recall a particular Maori family with whom he was working. The man in this family had had a terrible accident. He'd been riding a bike and a drunk driver had hit him and knocked him off his bike. He was totally innocent and was now substantially disabled. He walked very strangely and was not able to work in the way that he could before. This accident had totally changed his life. It was a chance event that just seemed very, very unfair. This man was really struggling to come to terms with the unfairness. He had a wonderful wife and neat kids and they'd given him considerable support. He came into therapy about two years after the accident because his partner had just about had enough and was thinking of leaving. It was a tragic situation. It made complete sense to me why this man couldn't cope and why he was so focussed on the unfairness of life. And it also made complete sense why his partner would be thinking of leaving. She had carried him through the period of the accident, and all the recovery period. She had hung in there with the kids, supported him, been really fantastic to him, and was now overburdened. The situation was just too much for her. In turn, he really loved his family and certainly didn't want them to go. Everybody was losing.

Now the obvious thing was to try and help this guy to move on in some way – to face the unfairness and acknowledge it but then to try to get on with life. And any number of people had tried to facilitate this, but nothing had worked. Warihi was sitting behind the one-way screen trying to work out the metaphorical reflection. He wondered if there was something there that could talk about rejuvenation in some way. He then went on to describe a famous indigenous tree, the totara. Most Maori carvings are from the totara tree. And there's a famous Maori proverb about the totara that Warihi evoked – 'whenever one totara falls another one grows in its place'. Building on this we crafted a metaphorical reflection which acknowledged the unfairness of the situation and also the strengths and actions that had been taken by all the family members. Warihi quoted the saying about the totara tree falling and a new one growing in its place. He then said straight out in front of the whole family, which I couldn't do with a Pakeha family but was certainly quite appropriate in this situation as Warihi is a Maori elder, 'I've seen the totara fall, but I haven't seen the new growth'. And he just left it at that.

A couple of weeks later the man came back. He walked in the room and looked straight at Warihi. There was no sense of politeness and he said 'I was so bloody angry with you last time'. Warihi was a bit taken back, and I thought 'I wonder what's going to happen here!' The man then said, 'I knew exactly what you meant. You're right, I died but there was no new life'. This guy had completely transformed in the meantime. He had begun re-building his life. This was a number of years ago and the family has gone from strength to strength since then.

What is it about the use of metaphor in this situation that you think was significant?

Charles: What's so important about metaphor is that it works its way beyond normal conversation and even beyond rationality in a sense. This metaphor evoked history and culture as it is a very old saying. It evoked the sacredness of life and spirituality. And it evoked the rhythm of the seasons, of life and death. In these ways it was congruent with the principles of belonging, sacredness and liberation. The use of metaphor can also protect people's prestige in a way that direct talk cannot. If Warihi had said something like, 'If you go on focusing on the unfairness of this situation you're going to lose this wife, you're going to lose your whole family' it would have gone nowhere. But a metaphor can land in a way that doesn't deplete the status of the person. I'm sure this is why it's used so much in Polynesian poetry. Metaphor can protect relationships while still communicating significant messages. In this situation Warihi used a metaphor that he sensed would resonate with the family due to its cultural context. He delivered it in the way he did because it was culturally appropriate as he is a Maori elder. All these sorts of considerations are important in this work.

We offer these metaphorical reflections and families can either take them up and make meaning with them or they can leave them. In my experience, if we've done our job properly, if we've created a reflection that resonates with the stories told by the family, then they will incorporate them into their lives in some way.

What are some of the other sorts of metaphors that are evoked in your conversations with families?

Charles: There are many types of metaphors that we evoke, such as natural images – of tributaries coming into rivers and becoming part of the mainstream, of sunsets. We also use lots of images in relation to culture woven mats, and other cultural crafts. And if children are involved then sometimes television characters are very useful – I recall a time when Thomas the Tank Engine was a metaphorical friend. Children's ways of being are often very metaphorical and we make use of this.

How do you use metaphor when you're with a number of family members who have quite divergent views on what's going on?

Charles: We would evoke a divergent metaphor. If we are talking with an educated Pakeha (European) family and we know they are interested in music, we might speak about an orchestra. We could speak about the wind section and the string section and the need for variation within both of these. We may also speak about how in order for an orchestra to be able to function there are points of co-ordination – these occur within gentle pastoral symphonies, and also within discordant pieces. We could also draw upon the analogy that different instruments play at different times wind instruments don't have to be playing all the time. Often they are not playing at all, and yet there are times when they're really highlighted. If the metaphor is richly described, and remains resonant with the family, it can sometimes address situations in which one voice is dominating and create space to acknowledge a diversity of voices.

Alternatively, if this sort of metaphor would not resonate with the particular family, we could turn to other images such as the colour of feathers. When you look closely at all the finer bits that make up the colour of a feather the diversity is extraordinary. We normally have feathers in our room that we can look to as a symbol of how a vibrant diversity of colours come together in one beautiful form. I think it's important to say again that we don't prepare these metaphors. They evolve from the conversations we have with the families. In ninety percent of the time the metaphor would grow from what a family member has said or alluded to in conversation.

I remember a Canadian family who had recently immigrated to New Zealand and who were struggling. We had just been in British Columbia and in our metaphorical reflection we spoke of the salmon that we saw on Vancouver Island that swam upstream. These salmon have an incredible strength to swim upstream every year. We built the whole struggle that the family was having around the metaphor of the salmon. At the end of the reflection, which we always read twice, the family was very moved. We discovered that the whole reason the family was in New Zealand was because the father was a fish scientist who had been brought out by the New Zealand government! He said, 'I've come here to help with the trout who do the same thing'. The trout and the salmon go up the rivers, against the current. It really drew the family together. These sorts of things can happen when using metaphor and when you are listening to the cues given by the family. These metaphors can then take on a life of their own.

As you are speaking I can see how the use of metaphor in these ways links people's lives to broader landscapes and histories. I can also imagine how the metaphor can then become a focus of meaning, a symbol through which families can understand their lives and imbue them with meaning. It seems as if you are engaging the family in making new meaning about life through the use of metaphor. How do you see this process playing itself out?

Charles: We have tried hard to break free from the language of medical metaphors and also to break from biological metaphors, systemic metaphors. We have found it far more helpful to create a language of hope. Metaphors contribute to this beautifully. All of our cultures are full of metaphors and stories about people, animals, natural events that evoke success through struggles. Religions and spiritualities also contain stories of hope and regeneration. When people come for therapy they are seeking change and are looking for hope in doing so. Metaphors often provide an opening to an alternative meaning. It is no good just to say, 'Okay, you've got this problem but there is hope'. This is just imposing meaning upon the family. It gives no scope for people to engage with their imagination and their own interpretations. But a metaphor can open new possibilities.

For instance, today, given that we are on one of the beautiful little islands of Samoa, we swam around for ages and for a time all we saw was dead coral ruined by the hurricane. But then we came across a patch of beautiful new coral and there were small tropical fish swimming around. It was a place of many different depths. The different colours of the coral and the fish were quite awesome. This experience could be used as a metaphorical reflection. If we used a metaphor like this it would be linked to the stories that the people had told us and the experiences we had together. It would be offered in a culturally appropriate manner. The moment of coming across the patch of beautiful coral and tropical fish would be linked to a moment in the conversation in which an alternative meaning was found. This could have been an important insight shared by a member or members of the family, or the certainty of achievement after a period of struggle. Metaphors can powerfully acknowledge what a family is going through and can also offer a strength to hang on to.

It is possible to use metaphors to land your messages gently. They can preserve people's status. They can also be non-judgmental and this is really important. We avoid metaphors that imply a moral imperative of any sort. Where there's a moral element people can so easily feel judged. Saying something like, 'Come on, hang in there' can imply a moral obligation and can breed resentment or a sense of failure. Metaphors can offer different possibilities. With them we can paint a picture of the struggle that the person's having, but paint it from a totally different perspective, one that leaves them without feeling obligated, and one that takes the story into a new realm of possibilities.

A metaphor that we have found helpful in explaining our role in therapy and in understanding the many perspectives that inform the creation of reality is that of a mountain. You can look at a mountain from the north or you can look at it from the east. From each perspective you gain a completely different view and yet it is authentically the same mountain. This idea can be very liberating for people. The reflections that we as therapists are offering are endeavouring to give an eastern view of the same situation that the family's been looking at from a northern view.

It is really interesting to me to consider therapy as a place in which metaphors are co-constructed and how these metaphors in turn open space for alternative meanings and preferred stories. Is this the sort of realm you see yourself working within?

Charles: Yes. The use of metaphor in therapy is sophisticated and at times subtle. Metaphors are representations or pictures of what we go through in life. They can capture people's hopes, loves, sorrow and struggles, in ways that offer new meaning. Our role is to make metaphors of sacredness, belonging and liberation more visible, to assist people to engage in meaning-making through metaphor, and at times to craft metaphors on which to float new meaning. We hope that these metaphors will be of assistance to those who are consulting us.

Reference

Campbell, W., Tamasese, K. & Waldegrave, C. 2000: 'Just therapy.' In *Family Therapy: The field's past, present and possible futures*, 1(1). Adelaide: Dulwich Centre Publications.

6.

Family therapy and the question of power

an interview with

Kiwi Tamasese

&

Charles Waldegrave

This interview was conducted by Ian Law.

*There have been significant debates in the history of family therapy as to the
usefulness or correctness of power as a concept. What meaning does that have
for 'Just Therapy'?*

Charles: I think that the movement away from power as a metaphor was a very
good movement. There were earlier family therapy writers who really defined
systemic thinking around issues of power. But the movement away from that
metaphor shouldn't detract from an analysis of power differentials that occur
between people of different cultures, those cultures that dominate other cultures
in our society. We at The Family Centre have always been interested in the
notion of power differentials. We study and analyse them endlessly because we
are committed to a 'just therapy', to social justice. Power is very important in
terms of analysing the difference, the injustice. For instance, men and women
aren't operating together in a neutral vacuum. There are definite power
differentials. So the whole notion of accountability developed at The Family
Centre relates to power differentials, such as cultural accountability and gender
accountability. We are interested in the analysis of power differentials, but not
power as a metaphor to describe families or as a helpful way to look at families.

*The notion of accountability seems to be central to your thinking, central to the
way that you would work with people. Would you care to expand on the notion of
accountability and its importance or relevance?*

Kiwi: What we are faced with daily at The Family Centre is the keen sense of
people's non-control of basic resources in their lives. Resources like housing,
schooling, and even control of the languages their children speak and learn at
school. So, while the whole idea of metaphors can be useful, they can also be
limiting as well, because they are only our description. It all depends how you
use them. Power can be about having control of a situation in a way that has
positive connotations, if, for example, people have control of their housing and
the language their kids learn to speak. Many people who come to therapists have
no control over these things. Often there is no parity between the families and the
therapists they see. Most families have no control of the process of therapy or
how their lives are denoted in therapy. They are simply directed through calm
conversation. Our ways of describing often suit our purposes as workers.

So, in terms of accountability, I think it is a way of saying that we are working in situations of unequal power, and therefore there must be a dialogue with a basis of some equality. So those who are in the dominating position must be prepared to expose the reasons behind their actions and decisions to those who are not in such a position. This can often be men to women, or dominating cultures to dominated ones.

It seems to me you are saying that metaphors may be helpful but, in a sense, are limiting and that the experience of powerlessness is real. So I'm wondering, then, in terms of changing meaning systems, how you take into account the structural issues of poverty and institutional racism?

Kiwi: I think what we try to do is to nominate the people's own strengths and to weave that in. We always try to help families move blame away from themselves to the people, policies, and decision-makers who are responsible for injustices they experience, like unemployment. There are preferred meaning systems and there are not-so-preferred meaning systems. The meaning system that affirms a family's survival of atrocious conditions and leads them on to self-determining goals will be a preferred meaning system, as opposed to meaning systems that adjust them to accepting the pain of having to live with it.

Charles: I think there is another angle on this. There are many attempts today in modern therapy, especially postmodern therapies, to address the issues of power between the family and the worker. They do this through reflecting teams or increasingly more 'democratic ways' of operating. There is, though, an incredible blind spot in the way that all these approaches operate within a prescribed Western European, North American, white, individualistic understanding. It doesn't seem to move from that to a more fundamental understanding of equality like the employment of workers from different cultures, the employment of different metaphors and concepts from those cultures, a movement away from individualism to communal-type thinking, a preparedness to stand aside from a lot of social science knowledge, which is basically one cultural way of describing events, and being prepared to address the spiritual meanings of cultures.

You really give away power when you respect the world of the groups who have been dominated, when they have their own properly resourced workers in their centres, and when those people have the space to create therapies that are relevant to the people of those cultures. They can then address the central issues of belonging, where people come from, which, in the vast majority of cases, are vastly different from the worlds that most of the therapists come from and are trained in. That's a real power issue. Most of the modern attempts at openness and the release of power are quite inappropriate to many of the powerless people, simply because they are an extremity of individual democracy that just doesn't make sense to people of a whole host of cultures. If the key proponents of many of these ideas actually began to enter into authentic cultural partnerships, they might do much more towards the sharing of that power differential, than they do by more and more attempts at individualised democracy.

How would you describe an authentic cultural partnership?

Kiwi: I think an authentic cultural partnership can only happen in situations where the culture that is oppressed names the terms of the partnership and operates within a frame where the work is in no way directed by the dominating culture.

Charles: And that raises status issues too. Like, the people are paid at an equal consultancy status; they have control over development of their own therapies; they are able to be accountable back to their own communities and not to other groups. Further, the issues they raise in working with their own people that come through in their therapy are picked up by the dominant culture. The dominant culture should then address their own issues and start being committed to breaking down the control among and beyond their own agencies, so that there really is an authentic partnership.

So, would you then call for an appreciation of the historical, political, social and cultural struggle of peoples, and see individuals or a couple or a family within that context?

Charles: Absolutely. That is true postmodernism, that is true 'story'. It's not a story around an individual and a particular problem that has been presented in therapy, which is the way most postmodernist narratives are being created. That's a story of people, and a story that really addresses the issues of pain in those stories. So that when people come from a particular culture, they come with a history from a collective of that culture, and that profoundly affects individuals. Of course there arc individual variances and differences in the story, but the history of those people is important. The collective cultural stories of peoples are really, really important, and significant to the essence of belonging and identity. In our view, healing, true healing, can only take place in that context.

Kiwi, in your plenary address to the Second Australian & New Zealand Family Therapy Conference (Melbourne 1991), I heard you talk about the idea that the problems of therapy are the symptoms of structural issues, such as poverty, and that you describe yourself more as a community worker than as a therapist. Could you talk some more about that?

Kiwi: [laugh] Well, actually I came into the field of family therapy through community development. The gifting of community development and community organising to family therapy is the analysis of contextual power differences, be they political or economic. It's a discipline that takes seriously the connection between the stories that the people bring to therapy and the stories that their people have lived out.

There is a detachment in family therapy of people from their genealogy of ancestry, their genealogy within their cultures, and their genealogy of societal placement. I think it has been very constricting of the discipline of family therapy, because what people go through is often defined as internal personal problems or functions of the family. They are not seen as a continuation of ancestry or ancestral genealogy.

Part of what you are saying is that if family therapy, and those who call themselves family therapists, continue to view families and individuals in isolation from their socio-political and cultural context, then they are only going to get part of the story.

Kiwi: They are only willing to get .005 of the story. What we must own within this planet is that we are diagnosing people out of .005.

Charles: In fact, maybe we can go a bit further than that and say that, if you are actually working outside that context – which most therapy in fact is – and if the problem that the family brings is associated with some external factor like housing, racism or sexism, then it's not that you're doing a minimal job in therapy, you're actually doing a pro-active, harmful job because you're separating yourself from that information. That will mean that the particular problem will return, perhaps worse, because you're consigning people back to the conditions that caused the problem in the first place.

That's really our concern – the denial in the field of the broad issues that people present. The avoidance of the context of pain is another. If people are in pain, the modern emphasis on solutions can be a great excuse for avoiding the pain. What we try to do is to track the pain, track it as the individual expresses it, track it in the family, in the community, in the culture, in the society, and address it all in that context. For us, if the problem is associated with unemployment or redundancy, it's as unjust not to name the political and economic planners that have structured unemployment into our society to lower inflation, as it is to not name a man's violence to a woman, and not name who is responsible for that, and who is innocent. People have the same experience of self-blame and depression. If you have a problem that is associated with something external, something structural in society, and you end up having your problem sorted out in therapy, you then go away believing that you were the author and creator of your problem, and that's an untruth. It perpetuates the powerlessness, the inadequacy and the lack of self-determination of whole groups of people. That is what has happened in most social welfare and psychiatric institutions in many modern industrialised states.

So this colonisation of ideas into other cultures would actually help to attribute responsibility for problems to individuals, whereas you would see responsibility for power differences and the effects of power and oppression as being beyond individual and beyond family, and much more located with social and economic planners?

Kiwi: If we don't, then in many therapeutic situations we simply make people invisible. Some of the most harmful effects of colonisation were the diseases, the killings, the subjugation – it's a long list. But alongside that, up to the modern day, colonisation is also about making a people and its language just disappear off the face of the earth by the non-telling of their stories, thus making their situation invisible. Family therapy is very famous for doing that – it just makes people's life stories invisible unless it's to help people to think about the situation as their own fault. That, too, was a very very apparent arm of colonisation, the defining of people in such a way that they actually think that what is happening to them now is their fault. But while they are screaming in self-blame, make sure that the cries never come out, just make them invisible enough. We make people invisible in family therapy by not connecting them to their genealogical stories and treating families of different cultures as if they came from the same history as your typical, middle class, European family, preferably from the Anglo-Saxon mould. By doing that *in* our field we are making people invisible, and therefore perpetuating a colonising practice.

Charles: It's even true if we are talking about white families. I think what we have learnt through this whole process, which is a latter learning, is that belonging is so important. That is, where you come from, who you belong to, what your history is, what our reflexes are, what are the ways that your family does things, how do they do death, how do they celebrate, how do they do these different processes of life, how do they celebrate birth, how do they experience all these various things, and the particular impacts of historical events on their culture.

The best therapy that we do as white people draws upon our own cultural metaphors. The making visible that which is invisible. At the heart of who we are is our identity, and our identity is tied up with who and where we belong. That's true for all people. If therapy begins to work from that perspective then it will relate to histories of people, to their cultures, and to the context of their stories. It will also relate to the societies in which they live and the resources which they have access to. That's not to say that all problems are necessarily to do with social justice, but it is the context that is quite central to many problems; I guess we would go as far as saying probably to the vast majority of problems.

Kiwi: It will affect the growth of the problem if it doesn't directly cause it. Our experience in working with marginalised people tells us that their experience of subjugation has resulted in what they experience now which, in turn, leads them to many therapists. For example, the experiences of drug and alcohol abuse that's rife among marginalised people.

Kiwi, I've heard you describe naming as being a political act, a therapeutic act, an act that would have costs and would take courage. You have also talked about how colonisation has rendered invisible much of the colonised or dominated culture's experience and knowledge. So when you talk about naming as apolitical act, would you see that as rendering the invisible visible?

Kiwi: Rendering the invisible visible. Rendering power to those who have been denoted as powerless. Encouraging their right to question what is right now. Encouraging the questioning of personalities and theories in the field and beyond in society. This is, actually, a political activity in that it questions decision-making and decision-makers. You can, of course, make a political decision not to make a political decision, and thus roll over.

So you would have a view that you cannot be apolitical. T o declare yourself apolitical would be a political act because it would maintain the status quo.

Kiwi: Definitely. An apolitical act is definitely a political act. To keep silent within the discipline of family therapy, knowing very well its constrictions, is a political act. But that political act is not so costly.

Which brings me to the question, what costs are there in naming and for whom?

Kiwi: I think you stand to lose credibility. You stand to lose a lot of credibility in naming and rendering visible the invisible. You are actually questioning people's theoretical constructs and, if you are naming from a marginalised position, you have taken more of a risk because they can actually block you out or block your voice out.

What costs to you, personally and collectively, and to the Centre as a community, would you have experienced in terms of your political stances in naming?

Kiwi: You stand to lose very close friendships at a personal level. Building friendships within the discipline of family therapy and questioning your own friends' theoretical constructs means that you stand to lose those personal friendships. Sometimes those personal friendships are very close supports and you are going to lose that. I knew that I just couldn't throw rocks without having any backup to what I was saying, so I've had to work really hard at knowing the details of most theoretical constructs before throwing them into question. So that costs a lot of sleep. We have had to take on major streams of practitioners and theoreticians, and when you do that you run the risk of them closing off resources and misnaming you. People like me run the risk of being discounted.

Charles: There is a cost to thinking on your own and not thinking with the mainstream, because this becomes offensive to those people who are comfortable. We are not just talking about ideas. We are talking about resources going to different people, employment going to different people, ways of thinking, taking into account knowledges that people didn't learn as social scientists, recognising and valuing the knowledge of people from cultures which you can't go out and learn. People get angry with those ideas.

I think that in our agency it's been extremely costly for the people of other cultures, particularly Maori and Samoan workers who, in order to validate what they are saying, have had to really expose whole elements of their own cultures and their own lives, simply to deal with armchair, non-involved thinking, and criticism. They often have to put themselves and their people's lives on the line. It's very costly.

The cost for those of us who have chosen to work with the people who most need the health and welfare resources is that it's very hard to fund the work, so you live in a continual financial deficit. You never have enough money because the people you are working with can't pay and that's why no-one's doing any work with them. That's costly because you can't have administrative support and back-up that other big organisations have.

I think that along with the costs we should also name the joys and the experience of authenticity in actually addressing real problems. The energy that's created in cultural and gender partnerships is really exciting. You can really feel you are a part of networks that are changing ways of thinking and making things better now. Addressing issues like patriarchy, racism, and poverty will hopefully contribute to making things better for the next generation.

It is true, though, that when we do good therapy then we go with families into their pain, and that can be costly. It's much easier to have a trendy technique or a fast solution. It's much more difficult to really honour the stories that people bring and to help facilitate some sort of liberation with it.

What part does accountability play in tins?

Charles: I think accountability is really central to all our work. We wouldn't need to have such procedures if we were able to solve all our problems of racial and gender bias, and the bias of privilege over poverty. Individual therapists usually feel they are not racist and I'm sure they're not at a personal level. I'm sure most therapists would not want to commit racist or sexist acts. But the social expectations, the professional groups and the institutional expectations privilege white and male values at the expense of women and dominated cultures. For men or white people to disregard this is to deny their relationship to the history of men and to the history of white people, and the responsibilities those collectivities have to change. At The Family Centre we often say that the best judges of injustice are the groups that have been unjustly treated. So we make all gender work in the agency, including men's groups, directly accountable to women, and all cultural work accountable to those cultures. We have developed procedures for this.

Spirituality and sacredness pervades everything you do, everything you talk about, and how you live your lives. How would you explain or describe the notion of spirituality and sacredness?

Kiwi: Within culture, people's lives, their struggles to live and to make something of themselves, are sacred. Because life is usually lived in struggle, people want to make sense of what is and what can be. The struggle to be should be regarded as something that is special, something that should be respected, and something that should not be tampered with. It not only involves a single life – that single life has come to be because of other lives.

I would say that we are here because somebody else struggled for us to be here, somebody else has gone without much for us, and therefore their struggle should always be remembered in our lives. Their lives are sacred and so are ours.

Each of the families that come to us come out of the stories of people who are trying to make sense of their lives and their situations, and that's sacred. Our meeting is spiritual in the sense that spirituality to us also encapsulates our knowing within our spirits. It becomes a meeting of the knowing of the family and knowing of the therapist of what they have been through. If we don't know then it's our problem – we should go and find out. Families come expecting respect because they are in pain, and offer themselves vulnerably to us for our care and whatever help we may be able to offer. It's a meeting of their knowing and our knowing, and if our knowing is impaired then we render our meeting non-spiritual. It is as though we are rendering the family non-present.

Charles: The social sciences, in their arrogance, are so cynical about spirituality. They can't measure or validate it through scientific process. Yet many cultures have not severed the relationship between body and soul in the way Western European and North American white cultures have. For those who have not, spirituality is fundamental to their view of life. This is a major reason why they have so little faith in therapy. They don't go unless they are forced to go by the Department of Social Welfare or the courts. People don't choose therapy, because it is experienced as a process that doesn't respect their soul. I'm using soul in the same sense as 'soul music', the depth of personality, sense of belonging, who we are, and where we come from – that sense of 'soul'.

But we don't really talk about spirituality in therapy. Rather, spirituality is a metaphor we choose to use of therapy. It is one of a number of metaphors that we use; weaving is another one. It helps us understand what we are doing, because the metaphor we use profoundly affects the way we act. When we use that metaphor we are not talking about Christian institutionalism, we are talking about the profound essence of being, and particularly about pain. People come to therapists because they are in pain – they are having difficulties and they become vulnerable and are exposed. They speak as we do when we talk about the deepest things that happen to us, to some close member of our family, or to a very close friend. Whenever we do that it is a very spiritual, energising experience. It's a very deep experience which is very dear to the friend or the relative and to us.

People come to therapists and have that same experience. That's why we say therapy is a sacred process. Because it is sacred, it's worthy of honour. People do not present problem pathologies that need to be removed through some scientific process. They share stories that need to be honoured, and so it's important to try and respond in the best tradition of spirituality, which is that of liberation. We try to encourage new meanings that facilitate resolution and hope. The sacred encounter we call therapy involves a family who share their vulnerability and pain, together with a therapist who facilitates liberation. The art of therapy is best judged by the quality of that sacred encounter.

I wanted to ask you, Kiwi, within this work and within the field of family therapy, what has been your experience as a Samoan, a woman, and a Samoan woman?

Kiwi: It's an area that I'm starting to think I should actually write up. I entered the discipline of family therapy with a lot of questions. I should, really, write down my first impressions of the discipline, [laugh] I remember first despairing when I came to The Family Centre. Charles first invited us to consider developing a Samoan family therapy project. I was very despairing. I thought, 'My God, nobody should ever go near family therapists' and, in fact, the name we termed therapists at the time was 'family terrorists'. That was because I, as a Samoan woman, did not see the discipline take serious account of people's own stories and what the families bring to us as therapists. I was very despairing of that for a long time. I was also very despairing of simple, basic human things, for example the assumption that we as therapists are untouched by what the people bring, as if healing was only a one-way process. We, the famous healers that we are, employ all healing modes and practices on people, and we somehow come out of the whole encounter unaffected. The non-naming of our experience seems to me to be very arrogant. There we were, in the midst of a family or a situation, and we came out of it unaffected and detached.

I thought, if we are detached because we are not listening to what the people are saying, we are very arrogant indeed. Because what they are saying through their conversations are some very gentle confrontations of our own knowledge and our own theoretical base. If we come away detached and unquestioning of that, we have not been open. I was despairing that the discipline's own energies were very focussed on the family *per se,* and not on the larger social political systems.

However, I got drawn to it because I had some really strong friends who were family therapists. They kept on raising the issue of what we do in our community development work when we come by issues of abuse, issues of domestic violence, people having psychiatric breakdowns, and I couldn't say as a community development worker, 'well, we're running around trying to change the policy of government, that will bring help'. For sure, that will bring help, but what do we do with people immediately who are facing distressing situations? I think, finally, that got me a bit more interested.

What hopes would you have?

Kiwi: For family therapy? Oh my God! [laugh] This time in Australia, like in the US and Canada, I have been really energised. I can see some changes coming into the discipline. People are really responsive. They are brave enough to start questioning their own theoretical constructs and change their practices. That is very encouraging.

Charles, what has been your experience of being white, being a man, a priest and a psychologist, amongst many other things, and your work as a therapist in The Family Centre?

Charles: All of those aspects are a part of what is me and a part of the class and groups and collectives of people that I belong to. That gives me a view of the world and it is important how I reflect on that and what responsibilities and commitments I take from the reflection.

Being a man, I've got to relate to the collectivity of manhood and what manhood is in relation to womanhood. There are obvious areas of injustice, inequity in the numerous histories of patriarchy. There are some very fine contradictions to that negative side but, nevertheless, the history of manhood in the culture that I come from is really not good in its relationship to womanhood. Like a lot of other men, I want to help change that. I don't want to do what woman workers do – it's not appropriate anyway. I and other men are involved in dialogue with groups of women in an endeavour to change our relationship to one that is just and satisfying for both of us.

Being white, and a privileged white at that, brings the same sort of challenge. I have to look at the collectivity of being white and the nature of the relationship of the collective of whiteness *(pakeha* as we call it in New Zealand) with Maori and Pacific Island people, and do something about that. I see therapy in the context of those collectivities. This doesn't seem to be very common. For me it's strange that it's not a common way in which people look at it. People don't seem to want to look at those collectivities, they don't want to look at histories, so much therapy is about individuals.

Being a priest and a psychologist, I try to do justice to those professions so that they don't continue to impose, and practice, social control. I look at how they can authentically fulfil the ideals that those professions also have in their stories to bring about liberation, a greater sense of equity, good health in society, and so on.

Can I ask you the question that I asked Kiwi, which is, what hope do you have for family therapy as a set of organising ideas?

Charles: I have hopes, but they are fairly idealistic. I'm really more concerned about the lack of initiative to move beyond the dominating white cultures. I hope that we can learn to talk the narratives of other cultures and to begin to relate authentically in ways of social justice. I think I have really more despair about that than I have hope. I do hope, though, that one day the health and welfare resources will actually get to the people who most need them. I hope they will be controlled, created and developed by the cultures and genders who are to benefit from them. I hope approaches will develop that are more creative, much richer, and more historical in content.

Finally, is family therapy as an organising set of ideas still helpful, or should we be looking more to community development work?

Charles: Families, one way or another, are here to stay. I use the term in the broadest sense. People are going to live in groups and they are going to be intimate in groups. Experiences of intimacy are always associated with both joy and sadness, so I think there will always be a need in that area. However, in order for family therapy to address that need, the field has got to take seriously the essence of that intimacy and the belonging that's involved. The quality and sacredness of human life that's captured in these groups is still poorly understood, in my view. Such understanding is in its infancy in the social sciences.

Kiwi: There will always be families, be they extended families, single parent families, gay families, or whatever. If our discipline, family therapy, does not take into consideration people's sense of belonging, and help people discover their centre of belonging, then it will render itself irrelevant to the struggles of many families. I think people will come up with another set of ideas, another notion that will be more relevant to their situation. We, in the discipline of family therapy, must work to find ourselves relevant in people's struggles to survive. We need to respond to family situations in a manner that enables people to make lives for themselves and the generations to come.

7.

The challenges of culture to psychology and postmodern thinking

by

Charles Waldegrave

This paper was originally published in M. McGoldrick ed. (1998) *Re-visioning Family Therapy: Race, Culture and Gender in Clinical Practice.* New York: Guilford Press. Republished here with permission. Copyright remains with Guilford Press.

Subjecting the assumptions that underpin the social sciences to a cultural analysis can be a disturbing experience, indeed. Such an analysis will confront the claims of the social sciences, and thus psychology, to knowledge that is independent, neutral, objective and verifiable (Weiten 1995; Habermas 1971). Furthermore, a cultural analysis challenges the claim to an international body of knowledge that is intercultural.

Consider, for example, the language and the metaphors that are used in clinical psychology. The medical metaphors with their words like diagnoses and cures, the biological metaphors with their systemic focus, and of course social science itself, is a metaphor modelled on the physical sciences, and positivist thinking (Harré Hindmarsh 1993). These all combine to create practitioners who search for objective diagnoses, objective causes, objective explanations, and objective cures. Many clinicians have become so attached, in fact, to the scientific metaphor that it is no wonder that psychiatry, psychology, and nursing for example, often rely primarily on the so called objectivity of chemical therapies to heal. They often diagnose only to sort out which chemistry to use. But even when therapy is not that of chemistry, it so often relies on category diagnoses, such as those set out in the Diagnostic and Statistical Manual of Mental Disorders (DSM) published by the American Psychiatric Association, and the so called scientific medical explanations and cures (Tomm 1990).

It is post-modern thinking in the European world that has challenged all that (Foucault 1971; Maturana & Varela 1980). Of course there has always been scepticism outside the European world to the cold positivist metaphors. Maori and Pacific Island people in New Zealand have seldom voluntarily used the services of therapy. Normally, it was only when they were directed by the Departments of Social Welfare, Justice, or a psychiatric hospital, that they attended. On the whole, these processes have been imposed on them. Faith in the system amongst poor Pakeha (European) has been rather questionable also. But the real challenge to the so called objectivity of the scientific approach within the European world, is with the post-modern developments and particularly critical post-modern thinking.

Post-modernism basically states, that events occur in the physical world, and people give meaning to those events. In this paradigm there is no objective meaning, and no objective explanation. For example, I could walk over to a Maori woman colleague and friend of mine and put my arm on her shoulder. We could take this as an event that has occurred in the physical world. Different people will give different meanings to that event. Some people might say it's a friendly gesture. Other people might say it's a patronising gesture. Some might say it's a racist gesture. Another person might say it's cross-cultural camaraderie. Another person could label it as violent. Another person could say it's intrusive and sexist. Someone else might say it's connecting closely, and so on. The point is that there is no objective reality in terms of the explanations of events that occur in the physical world.

There are problems with this view, though, as it can suggest that all explanations are simply of equal value. But that is often not the case. The Jewish and Polish experience and explanations and of the Second World (European) War offer quite different meanings, than the Nazi explanations and meanings of those same events, and we would want to treat them differently. The victim/survivors of abuse often give different meanings to the physical events of their abuse than many perpetrators do. We would want to talk critically about the difference in those meanings.

So critical post-modernism talks about preferred meanings (Giroux 1983; Waldegrave 1990; Harré Hindmarsh 1993; Tamasese & Waldegrave 1993), meanings that emerge out of values. For example, we would want to say that gender equity is preferable to male dominance, or that cultural self-determination is preferable to monocultural dominance. Whatever position we take, flavours our view of the world. If there is no objective meaning, simply explanations of meaning, then we have to start assessing our values and ethics in relation to these meanings, particularly when we work with individuals, or a family. The issue of our values becomes essential.

The contribution made by post-modernism is the view that all constructions of reality are simply that. They are *constructions,* and that includes the social sciences. In fact, we could go further and assert that the social sciences simply offer one *cultural* description of events that occur in the physical world. That particular cultural explanation springs out of a world view that centres around concepts of individualism and secularism, which are dominant values in Western Europe and white North America. There are, in fact, many other cultural explanations and descriptions of events. This kind of perspective is a critical post-modern stance, and the sort of stance that we are very involved with at The Family Centre.

Many people remember the days when sexual and violent abuse was looked upon by psychologists, and other therapists, in clinical terms within the old medical, biological, and social science metaphors. Causes were sought, symptoms were treated, but the abuse was often ignored or considered outside the clinical arena.

Numbers of women politicised the issue however, and clarified the meaning they gave such events (Bograd 1984; Goldner 1985; Pilalis & Anderton 1986; McKinnon & Miller 1987; Kamsler 1990). Psychologists and therapists can no longer act as they did before. The *'abuse'* and the meanings we now give it have changed our practice and our explanations, not to mention the law. The tired old positivist metaphors were simply inadequate to the task. In fact, they contributed to a lot of unethical behaviour. It is the change of meaning, to a *preferred* meaning, that has made the difference. This was not discovered scientifically, it was the result of a political movement that created new awareness by drawing attention to the meanings we gave these events.

Bearing all this in mind, social scientists and clinicians should be more humble in their claims to knowledge. There is very little that we actually know. Take for example, schizophrenia; we don't really know what it is, or how to treat it, but we're very good at labelling people with it. In fact, we know very little in the social sciences about mental health. We've had few successes, in real terms. Failure is more characteristic of our work in mental health institutions, in prisons, and in welfare. The record is quite appalling. It could be said, there is no evidence to show that exorcism, traditional healing, or faith healing is any less successful in its work within the communities embracing such practices.

With that backdrop, let us consider some of the issues that cultures bring. Cultures are all about the meanings people give events. They raise critical issues for psychologists, issues like identity and belonging. Our experience at The Family Centre, working in an organisation, that is structured on cultural lines, in the fields of family therapy, community development, social policy research and education, has led to many new learnings. We work from three cultural sections, Maori, Pacific Island and Pakeha (European), each with workers from those cultures. These are some of our learnings.

Ideas of self versus family

All cultures carry with them history, beliefs and ways of doing things. Cultures particularly carry meanings. We experience practically all the most intimate events in our life, within a culture or cultures. Within our families or intimate groupings, we learn the rules and the accepted ways of doing things. Public life is also determined by the meanings created by cultures. This is very significant, and indicates that anyone working with people from a culture, different from their own, requires at least a qualitative appreciation and informed knowledge of that culture. Normally the only way you get that is by being a part of that culture, or at least being extremely familiar and under some supervision from someone of that culture.

This is often misunderstood by white people. It is often misunderstood, because most of us in white cultures seldom reflect on our base values, and how much our culture is permeated with the concepts of individualism. Most of the psychological theories, for example, have been developed in western Europe, and white North America. In those cultures, as with Pakeha (European) New Zealand, individual self-worth is very important. Indeed, for practically all clinical psychological and psychotherapeutic theories, the primary goal of therapy is that of *individual self-worth.* That is because destiny, responsibility, legitimacy, and even human rights, are seen to be essentially individual concepts. Concepts of self, individual assertiveness and fulfilment are central to most of these therapies.

If, on the other hand, you come from a communal or extended family culture, questions of self-exposure and self-assertion are often confusing and even alienating. I remember when I was involved in a project with the Pacific Island Section. We were talking and debating about the whole concept of *self* in psychotherapy and psychology. One of the workers said: 'You don't realise what it is like for me as a Samoan, when I'm asked a question like "what do *you* think?" about something in therapy. It is so hard for me to answer that question. I have to think: what does my mother think, what does my grandmother think, what does my father think, what does my uncle think, what does my sister think, what is the consensus of those thoughts – ah, that must be what I think.' That is the way he described it. He explained that for him it was an unnatural question, and an extraordinarily intrusive question.

Questions relating to self often alienate people. They crudely crash though the sensitivities in communal based and extended family cultures. Among individually based cultures, such questions can be quite appropriate. Outside these cultures, however, the questions are often experienced as intrusive and rude. They can rupture co-operative sensitivities among people, and destroy the essential framework for meaning which should be drawn upon for healing.

Some examples in our own practice may help illustrate this. At the Family Centre, when the Maori Section first decided to develop a Maori therapy, they invited me to dialogue with them. Early in the project, there was a situation where a couple were referred from the Family Court. The issue concerned a custody and access dispute. In those days at the Family Centre there was one Maori worker, Warihi Campbell. He was working as a Maori consultant behind a one way mirror. That has all changed now, and there is a whole Maori Section that does all their own work, but these were the early days.

Warihi and I worked behind the mirror. There was a Pakeha (European) therapist in front with the family. We had all met and been introduced before the interview. It became clear that the mother (and wife) in this family had left, and the father (and husband) was in the family home with their children. The issue of dispute centred around the mother wanting to get back into the house with her children, and wanting the father out.

As we began to talk, it became clear that the father was quite happy for that to occur. Both of them had a lot of experience in the parenting of the children, and both were considered responsible and capable in those areas. The therapist, after discussion for quite some time, discovered that there was one hitch. The maternal grandmother wanted the children and the father to stay in the house together. As the discussion continued, the therapist operating from a Pakeha (European), individualistic perspective, recognised the parents as the primary decision-makers, said, 'Well, if you two agree for this shift, then why don't you (to the father) just move out, and you (to the mother) can move in with your children. Then you can sort of explain it to your mother.'

When the therapist made that move, Warihi became very concerned and tapped on the window to bring the therapist behind with us. He stated that in Maoridom the primary relationship traditionally is between grandparent and grandchildren, not between parent and child as in most Pakeha (European) cultures. 'If in fact you go against the grandmother's wishes, and she will have reasons for wanting this, then you run the risk of alienating this family from the extended family. She is not here to give her reasons. You must not do that.'

We had agreed in this project from the earliest days, that there would be no questioning of any of this sort of cultural direction. So, the therapist was sent in to say what Warihi had said. As soon as that was said, the couple agreed, because they understood the wisdom behind it. They were Maori and it made sense to them. The custody-access situation was solved from that moment onwards. In fact, in time things changed, and the grandmother, a year or two later, was quite supportive of a variation in that arrangement.

After the interview, we reflected on what had happened, and the psychologists among us realised that we were never taught anything like this in our clinical training. We recognised, that had we gone against that grandmother's wishes, it would have been very disruptive for that family. It may well have alienated them from members of their whanau (extended family). We had never thought of that before. It would have caused much the same problems for them, as if we disregarded the wishes of a parent in a Pakeha (European) family, and simply agreed to a grandparent's view. For most Pakeha (European) that would be experienced as extremely inappropriate and insensitive. We then began to think of how many times that must have happened. If you're not part of the culture, it is something you know nothing about, normally. If you are part of it, it is quite natural.

We then began to think how many times this must have happened in the Justice Department's psychological work, in the mental health area and so on. How many times, with the best of intentions these sorts of things must have occurred. This is because the cultural knowledge has not been seen to be significant in clinical work (Waldegrave 1985; Durie 1986; Boyd-Franklin 1989; Waldegrave & Tamasese 1993; McGoldrick 1994).

Respect, shame and spirituality

Another aspect that has stood out in these projects has been the different notions of respect in therapy. I think amongst most educated Pakeha (European) people, there is a feeling that everyone is the same. There is a liberal approach. We actually don't treat everyone the same, but we try to in therapy. We often avoid attaching respect to status in an obvious way. For example, parents with teenagers or adolescents often come in for help, and are really upset about what is happening at home, or what perhaps the young person is doing. It is quite common in a Pakeha (European) situation to hear the parents concerns respectfully, and then turn to the young person, and say, 'Well, Johnny or Jenny, you heard what your Mum and Dad have said, what are your views?' I have noticed whenever that same question is asked of a Maori or Pacific Island young person, they just lower their eyes and become silent. This is because they are being asked to comment and evaluate what the generation above them has said. This individualises them and discourages the respect they are taught between the generations. If a young person's opinion on these matters is wanted, there are different processes for gaining that information.

The whole issue of communal shame, especially in areas of abuse, is also a major issue. For example, the process of identifying a person who has been a perpetrator of abuse in a family is quite different. If this is approached directly with a family, the whole whanau (extended family) experiences the shame, including the victim/survivor. As a result the total family often becomes silent. Although it can be quite appropriate to be direct in this manner with a Pakeha (European) family, because it is acceptable to individualise blame, in Maori and Pacific Island families it can further victimise the survivor of abuse. Where identity is experienced collectively, the implications of many therapeutic probes are quite different. There are, of course, acceptable ways of addressing these issues with perpetrators of abuse, but the route is different.

Spirituality is another important aspect that stands out. Social science prides itself in being a secular science. It is suspicious of anything other worldly. Families in these other cultures often share dreams, prayers and numinous experiences that are important to the life of the family and the issues of health and wholeness. When violations are being talked about, there is often a need for spiritual rituals of protection. Those important things that are considered sacred, are often totally disregarded by social scientists and psychologists.

Effects of the predominance of western fundamental values

We often illustrate some of the significant differences, between Pakeha (European) fundamental values and Maori and Pacific Island values in the following way:

Communal	/	Individual
Spiritual	/	Secular
Ecological	/	Consumer
Consensual	/	Conflictual

From an ecological perspective, people's relationship to the environment is very different if they see Mother Earth in terms of who they are and where they stand, as opposed to an investment to be exploited or developed for profit.

Although many Pakeha (European) people are environmentally conscious, the values of consumerism predominate. Currently the pressures of consumerism, and privatisation are increasingly influencing our health services, for example.

In the Pakeha (European) world we often underestimate how confrontational the institutions of our society are. Our political party systems are set up, so that one party puts up a thesis, and the others knock it down. The arrangement in the work places, between employers and employees, is confrontational also. This is quite different from Maori and Pacific Island consensual decision making institutions and structures, like the marae (traditional gathering place for Maori).

The social sciences have grown in an environment where these were central values. Naturally these values permeate the theories and training. Nowadays, nations and cultures, which have quite different values, are expected to qualify their clinicians and research personnel in the western approach. In countries like New Zealand the Accident and Rehabilitation Compensation Corporation (ACC) expect people from cultures that relate to communal, spiritual, ecological and consensual values to gain qualifications in academia that emphasise opposite values. This is quite absurd. It is particularly absurd when you consider that people in western cultures are actually searching for many of these values, themselves, at the moment.

In most western countries, people in indigenous and other cultural groups, who wish to enter one of the helping professions, are expected to gain a qualification in the social sciences to be recognised. Because of the dominance of white values in the social sciences, this often requires people to leave their people and values to study under other people with different values, in order to be qualified to work with their own people again. This sort of learning process is quite disrespectful to other cultures, and worse still may contribute to disabling indigenous and other cultural workers to help their own. For social science to become consistently relevant to people of these cultures, it needs to be developed by them within their own cultural frames.

Conclusion: The need for a Just Therapy

In summary, from our perspective at The Family Centre, the social sciences offer one cultural way of describing events. This is not to suggest that Pakeha (European) people are never communal, spiritual, ecological or consensual, but that the predominant values in most white cultures are individual, secular, consumerist and conflictual. These are also patriarchal values. That is because, until recently, men alone controlled the developments of science, technology, the markets and institutions of industrialised countries. These are the values in which the social sciences developed.

Cultures differ greatly from each other. People from different cultures have different histories. They can have different experiences of immigration or war trauma. The languages of different cultures promote certain concepts and reduce others. Definitions of what is acceptable and unacceptable behaviour differ from culture to culture. Associated concepts of respect and shame differ. Patterns of thinking and communication (i.e. linear patterns, circular patterns and so on) differ from culture to culture. The degree of affirmation and the degree of subjugation that a culture has experienced impact very differently on the feelings of belonging, identity and confidence, that the people from such cultures have. Family structures, boundaries, and decision-making differ from culture to culture. Culture probably is the most influential determinant of meaning that exists. That is because cultures express the humanity and co-operation of large groups of people over long periods of time. As such, they are sacred and worthy of the greatest respect.

Therapies and psychological practices that do not address cultural meaning webs in informed ways are racist. This may not be intentional, but the dominant values, from the group that controls all the other institutions in society, predominate in a manner that simply continues the process of colonisation. These days, colonisation is not carried out through the barrel of a gun, but through the comfortable words of those who change the hearts, minds and spirits of people. Therapists and teachers have a huge responsibility here. Psychologists, especially those in clinical practice, need to be aware of the significance of their influence.

We, in the social sciences, should know this. We were taught that belonging and identity are the essence of health and human potential. It has been convenient for us to deny this, but the results have been tragic. Those most in need of the health and welfare resources in our societies come disproportionately from cultures that are dominated. They deserve, at the very least, sensitive professional work that allows them to feel culturally safe.

Someone, after a workshop in New Zealand, once said to us, 'You know a Maori, if he or she want to, they can always learn to be a psychologist, but a psychologist can't learn to be a Maori'. Cultural knowledge may or may not be accompanied by social science knowledge. Cultural knowledge can stand on its own. Those who possess it, and choose to work in the helping professions, have gifts our countries desperately need. Our organisations require such people, and they need to be properly resourced, have employment security and control over their work. Other cultural work away from our organisations, also requires adequate resourcing. They can heal their own in ways that we will never be able to. Furthermore, they will almost certainly offer the field rich alternative metaphors and meanings that can free us from the tired old medical, biological and social science ones.

There is a unique opportunity for psychologists and other helping professionals to recognise other ways of describing events, which will lead to creative practices and enable the health and welfare resources to get to those who most need them, on their own terms. It would also enable other people, other workers from other cultures to develop new paradigms, and new shifts in our field. This will not lead to the abandonment of social science, but it will enable that body of knowledge, to sit appropriately along side other realms of knowledge, such as gender knowledge, and cultural knowledge, without dominating. A new experience for the social scientists, but I suspect a liberating one!

References

Bograd, M. 1984: 'Family systems approach to wife battering: A feminist critique'. *American Journal of Orthopsychiatry*, 54 (4):558-568.

Boyd-Franklin, N. 1989: *Black Families in Therapy: A multisystems approach.* New York: Guilford.

Durie, M. 1986: *Maori Health: Contemporary issues and responses.* Auckland: Mental Health Foundation of New Zealand.

Foucault, M. 1972: *The Order of Things: An archaeology of human sciences.* New York: Vintage Books.

Giroux, H. 1983: *Theory and Resistance in Education: A pedagogy for the opposition.* London: Heinemann.

Goldner, V. 1985: 'Feminism and family therapy.' *Family Process*, 24:31-47.

Habermas, J. 1971: *Knowledge and Human Interest,* trans. J.J.Shapiro. Boston: Beacon Press.

Harré Hindmarsh, J. 1993: 'Alternative family therapy discourses: It is time to reflect (critically).' *Journal of Feminist Family Therapy*, 5(2):2-28.

Kamsler, A. 1990: 'Her story in the making: Therapy with women who were sexually abused in childhood.' In C. White & M. Durrant (eds): *Ideas for Therapy with Sexual Abuse.* Adelaide: Dulwich Centre Publications.

McGoldrick, M. 1994: 'Culture, class, race and gender.' *Human Systems: The journal of systemic consultation and management,* 5(3-4):131-153.

McKinnon, L. & Miller, D. 1987: 'The new epistemology and the Milan approach: Feminist and socio-political considerations.' *Journal of Marital and Family Therapy,* 13(2):139-155.

Maturana, H. & Varela, F. (eds) 1980: *Autopoesis and Cognition: The realisation of living.* Boston: Reidel.

Pilalis, J. & Anderton, J. 1986: 'Feminism and family therapy: A possible meeting point.' *Journal of Family Therapy,* 8(2):99-114.

Tamasese, K. & Waldegrave, C. 1993: 'Cultural and gender accountability in the "just therapy" approach.' *The Journal of Feminist Family Therapy,* 5 (2), Summer. Reprinted in *Dulwich Centre Newsletter,* Nos. 2&3, Adelaide, Australia.

Tomm, K. 1990: 'A critique of the DSM.' *Dulwich Centre Newsletter,* No.3.

Waldegrave, C. 1985: 'Mono-cultural, mono-class, and so called non-political family therapy.' *Australia and New Zealand Journal of Family Therapy,* 6(4):197-200.

Waldegrave C. 1990: 'Just therapy.' *Dulwich Centre Newsletter,* 1:5-46.

Waldegrave, C. & Tamasese, K. 1993: 'Some central ideas in the "just therapy" approach.' *Australia and New Zealand Journal of Family Therapy,* 14(1):1-8.

   - 1994: Reprinted in *Social Work in Action,* eds. R. Munford & M. Nash. Palmerston North, New Zealand: Dunmore Press.

   - 1994: Reprinted in *Human Systems: The journal of systemic consultation and management,* 5(3&4).

   - 1994: Reprinted in *The Family Journal* (The official journal of the International Association of Marriage and Family Counsellors), 2(2), April.

Weiten, W. 1995: *Themes and Variations, 3rd Ed.* Pacific Grove, California: Brooks.

Spirituality

8.

Grappling with a contemporary and inclusive spirituality

by

Charles Waldegrave

This paper was originally delivered as a keynote address at the 'International Narrative Therapy & Community Work Conference' in Adelaide in February 2000.

It takes us rather a long time to say hello in New Zealand! I come from a team of women and men from three different cultures, and it is our custom on these occasions to greet people in a Pacific way.

First in Maori, the language of the indigenous people of our land of Aotearoa/New Zealand: *Whakamoemiti kite Atua mo nga manaakitanga me nga awhina kia matou. Te tangata whenua i tenei wa, Tena koutou. Nga mihinui kia koutou. Nga rangatira me nga whanau awhina, Tena koutou, Tena koutou, Tena koutou katoa.* Firstly, I thanked the source and spirit of life for the many ways we have been helped, and the hospitality of this gathering. Secondly. I greeted the indigenous people of this land and acknowledged their welcome to us, and finally I greeted you all as elders who bring health to families.

In Samoan: *E faatalofa atu i le paia lasilasi ua faatasimai.* I have greeted you in the deepest sacrificial sense of love, acknowledged your own sacredness, and wished you as elders the fullness of Pacific life.

And in our third language, which I assume all of you can understand, greetings to you all from our colleagues at The Family Centre. We would like to congratulate the Dulwich Centre organisers of this conference for their foresight and courage in giving this topic of *spirituality* such prominence this morning.

Spirituality posed a considerable problem for us at The Family Centre. We had formed a cultural partnership of Maori, Pacific Island and Pakeha (European) workers and developed an agency that was determined to honour the cultures, address our colonial history and develop new expressions of equity. Spirituality posed a major problem for us, because in the European world it is largely viewed as a personal matter that has no role in the work place. Whereas for our Maori and Samoan colleagues it was inconceivable to consider health and wellbeing as ever being disconnected from overt expressions of spirituality.

As we reflected on our different histories and traditions around spirituality, we began to understand the complexity of our problem. For example, for most of the cultures whose origins are in western Europe, the concepts of body and soul have been separated. Spirituality has been compartmentalised away from everyday life. It is widely accepted as a sort of perfectly acceptable optional extra out of working hours, for those who are interested in it, but public, professional and working life is viewed as being secular. The roots of this separation of concepts of body and soul have a long history in western thinking going back to Greek Platonic thought.

Our Maori and Pacific Island colleagues, however, have made it clear that the concepts of body and soul for them are integrally interconnected. Furthermore, they are connected to land and the environment. They explained a holistic perspective that saw compartmentalisation as an anathema. It was inconceivable to them to think of healing or any sort of care for people without spirituality being an integral part.

This posed a problem for all of us trained in the social sciences, because we were taught that secularism (i.e. a worldly or material view rather than a religious or spiritual view) offered a neutral position. In other words, by not expressing overt spirituality, we were respecting everyone's right to their personal beliefs. This fitted well with the scientific view that reality is only that which can be verified or measured.

This view was sorely challenged at our centre as Maori and Samoan workers stated that secular rules actually comprised a religious oppression on them. Secularism is not neutral in this sense. It is at one end of the continuum of spirituality (i.e. non-spirituality), and if imposed, oppresses other explanations of health and wellbeing on other parts of the same spirituality continuum. In other words, in the name of secular neutrality, our Maori and Samoan colleagues were prevented from both expressing their holistic approaches to care within their own community, and also from shared expressions of spirituality within the agency they worked.

To put it simply, we had a choice of expressing the status quo by continuing to impose the European secular view of work and other public places, and in doing so override the calls of our Maori and Samoan colleagues to a holistic view, or we could discover a collective approach to spirituality that we could all feel comfortable with. We chose the latter, because so much of our colonial history in New Zealand has involved disregarding and overriding Maori and Pacific cultural perspectives, and thus denied the possibility of an authentic partnership.

If we wanted to be able to relate authentically across cultures, we simply could not ban the deepest expressions and definition of health, wellbeing and relationship that two of our three cultures adhered to. Furthermore, we could not exclude ourselves from sharing with them, if we wanted to be genuinely in relationship together.

We had to address the deep fear within ourselves that any expression of spirituality by us in a work place would be seen as an imposition on others or even proselytising. We all prided ourselves as liberal thinkers and wanted no part of that. Nevertheless, we dearly wanted to enter into genuine relationships with our colleagues and we wanted to do so in a manner that honoured their cultural expressions and meanings.

The dilemma was to discover ways of speaking about and joining around notions of spirituality in a manner that enabled all of us to freely express that which each of us held dearest, and at the same time allow those of us from a western tradition to feel comfortable with its breadth and freedom from imposition on others. It became important for us to come up with some common understandings about spirituality and its meaning. This began an exploration.

The following offers a crystallisation of our thoughts. They are simply offered as our reflections, not the 'right' reflections, not the 'only' reflections, and certainly not the 'definitive' reflections. They are just part of our journey at The Family Centre.

✦   Spirituality to us is essentially about *relationship*. For us relationship is expressed in four primary ways. The first of these is the primary relationship between *people and the environment.* By this we refer to the land, the mountains, the sea, the sky and so on. Anything that promotes or facilitates the relationship between people and the environment, to us, is spiritual. Anything that detracts from this relationship, to us, is the antithesis of spirituality. For example, we would consider the environmental work of a green activist as spiritual, regardless of their personal beliefs, including atheism. We would affirm the work itself as spiritual because of the attention given to the land. Of course, they may have their own different understandings, and we would not seek to impose our view upon them. But to us, work that is facilitating the relationship between people and the land, the mountains, the sea, and the sky is spiritual.

In our experience, Maori, whenever they introduce themselves, introduce their mountain and their river. It is just a part of saying who they are. In the Samoan Mental Health Project that we have recently been involved in, participants spoke so clearly about how, if there is something going wrong with the land, then it affects people's minds. Within these cultures there is no cut-off point between individuals, their extended family and the land. Within western European traditions there are also a number of ways in which people's relationship to the environment is considered a realm of spirituality.

The second relationship we understand to be spiritual is that between *people and other people in terms of justice and love*. Whenever people are practising justice and love, whether it is in a household, in a community, in a nation, or internationally, it is spiritual to us. Any act of kindness, any act of love, any act of beauty, is an act of the sacred. We talk about justice *and* love because justice without love can be harsh, and love without justice can be sloppy and even unjust. Within this view, we place deep significance on acts of justice and love that address issues of equity in the realms of gender, culture, poverty, class and other forms of marginalisation. The opposite, of course, is the antithesis of spirituality.

The third relationship we focus on is that between *people and their heritage*, their ancestry, their forefathers and mothers, those who have gone before. That which honours people's heritage is spiritual in our view, and that which denigrates it is the opposite. Everybody has a unique sense of cultural belonging, including everyone of European heritage. We are all a part of the long history of our families. For some, the knowledge is difficult to access, but most people can go back at least one and usually two generations. Even where it is impossible to track down a lineage, we all have a heritage, a place from where we come, a land, a people, family. In some cases there is a shameful element, because their ancestors committed terrible acts against other people. That will not be the total story of the people involved, however, and a later generation can help right the wrongs by owning their heritage and working to transform it in the present. Within therapy there are so many conversations about identity and belonging, because they address the core of who we are and thus provide the basis of much of our health.

The final relationship we speak about concerning spirituality is between *people and the numinous*. We cannot find a better English word than numinous for that which is other, beyond, transcendent, or what some people call God. For us, that which affirms connections beyond the physical seeing, touching, measurable environment to the numinous is spiritual. That which works against this and defines the material, measurable world as the sum total of significant life, is to us, the antithesis of spirituality.

With this understanding of spirituality, we have been able to both share together and feel comfortable despite our very different cultural heritages. It obviously does not require people to sign up to any institutional religious body, although some choose to. There is space for traditional beliefs, and the wide range of spiritualities practised by people. There is also space for those who have difficulty addressing the numinous, but feel okay to share about the beauty of nature, a poem, some cool music, or whatever. This spiritual understanding has become the basis for our meeting together briefly most mornings and many of our discussions and debates. It also informs much of our practice and work life together.

Spirituality has also offered us a new language to describe our therapeutic work. We have abandoned many of the medical and biological metaphors commonly used to describe therapy. We define therapy as a *sacred exchange*. Sacred in the sense of 'the sacredness of life', or as having soul as in 'soul music'. People come to us who are deeply vulnerable and tell us stories that, if they were happening in our lives, we would only tell our closest friends and people whom we deeply trust. For us, that is a sacred gift that they offer. As therapists, we listen deeply, no matter how strange it may sound, honour the story and analyse the web of meaning that has created the problem. Then, in the best spirit of liberation, facilitate new and transformative meanings that inspire hope and reconciliation. This is the sacred exchange that we use to describe therapy.

In this way, a notion of sacredness has become the primary metaphor of our work. By using spirituality as our central image for an exchange within the therapeutic process, we reckon we are much more likely to treat people with a greater respect than if we applied the more commonly used mechanistic descriptions of casework.

These offer a few examples of our attempts to involve spirituality in a holistic and inclusive sense into our work, in a manner that respects the integrity of the three cultures, and inspires our views of the quality of humanity and the sacredness of human life. It has certainly deepened the quality of our relationships and helped us to express together in the work place, the sort of relationships we are endeavouring to facilitate in therapy.

Closing

Warihi Campbell and Kiwi Tamasese then closed this plenary session on Spiritualities with a similar degree of care with which they opened it – thanking the speakers for sharing with us their stories of what it is that they hold sacred in their lives.

9.

A spiritual prison tale

by

Warihi Campbell

There were two Maori men up in the prison, young men in their twenties. The social worker called me in to see them. The prison psychiatrist believed they were mentally ill – they were very disturbed and were 'seeing things' – and he had made arrangements to transfer the boys to the psychiatric hospital the following day. So I went up to see these men, and I took a Pakeha priest to accompany me. The psychiatrist was there too. They were in an underground cell. It seems that a man had once been hanged in that cell. They could see the spirits of that man and they were very afraid. I took some water from the tap and blessed it, and I sprinkled it over the boys and over the room, and said some prayers. I told the spirit that it had no business being there and to leave the men alone.

The next day the prison psychiatrist rang me and said, 'There's nothing wrong with those men now tell me what you did'. I said, 'You saw what I did', and I was so angry. He was from a European country somewhere, and I felt like saying 'Why don't you go back to your own country. There are plenty of unemployed Maori people who could do these jobs better than you.' You see, if Maori are mentally ill, you should have an understanding of the culture when you work with them to enable them to heal, but the Pakeha doctors just put drugs into their bodies.

Anyway, the only side effect of my treatment was that the two Pakeha men who were sharing the cell complained that my holy water had wet their beds!

Maori ways

10.

In the beginning

by

Warihi Campbell & Flora Tuhaka

The first Maori worker to be engaged as a cultural consultant and then Family Therapist was Warihi (Wally) Campbell. An Anglican priest, Wally had extensive experience working with Maori youth and gangs and was extremely knowledgeable about Maori affairs and culture. When his people first decided that it should be he who joined The Family Centre, Wally had no clear idea what the job was about. Wally was a gift from the local Maori people, binding them and the agency together as long as he was respected and well treated. They said if he was not, then they would take him back.

This is Wally's story of his first days at The Family Centre:

Charles had already been looking into the Maori people's world. His work as a priest had taken him into the Maori community to conduct services. He had observed how Maori people came together and wanted to change the Agency to make it more relevant to the Maori people. When I joined the Agency, it was a real Pakeha agency, When they first asked me to observe a family in therapy, I thought it was like Star Wars – a game of luck and win. It was so technological – one way screens, video cameras. I laughed, but I was pissed off, angry. They were only coping with their culture and Pakeha academic skills. I said to myself 'tomorrow I'm going to change this place. One of the things that struck me as so strange was that all the workers used to bring their own individual cut lunches. I decided I'd bring along my big pot of kai (food) and put it in the middle of the table, and if they didn't accept my pot of kai, I was going to take myself home. It was one way to test the Agency. I put my lovely pot of kai on the table and told them they could help themselves to it. It was to show my way of working with people – sharing, offering hospitality. After that the lunch habits changed, and we now have an account to pay for food when guests arrive, and we all eat communally. It's an important part of our sharing. It's good to have a nice building, but it's no good without people. I'm a priest, I know a lot of people, and they began to come to the Agency. But after some years, Kiwi and I were getting overloaded. There were issues – rape, violence – that need women's insight and leadership, so I gave them the challenge for a Maori woman to join me. So we found the funding and Flora came.

Flora Tuhaka joined The Family Centre in 1986. She is a People's Warden of the Maori Pastorate, and a member of the Wainuiomata Marae Komiti (meeting house committee). She too has extensive experience of working with the Maori Community and works at the Agency as a Family Therapist and Community Worker. The following is her account of coming to work at the Centre:

The Maori and the Pakeha approach differed very much in the way they greeted families. For the Maori what is crucial is that you find a connection. It is important first to talk about genealogy, because in the beginning our ancestors were all connected to each other. If you know their ancestors and they know yours, then you can find the thread which connects you to them. It is important to find that connection, because then you are not a stranger and people can talk. It is important too, when working with Europeans – find the connection, and then people can talk.

I work in the way that would be comfortable for my people. It helps them to unwind and tell their stories. It is the quality of the relationship between you and the family that is the most important – how well you have been able to link up with people. It is important for our people to keep our links together. When people have come for therapy, we believe that their troubles and problems are left here, so that when we meet them in the street they are greeted and acknowledged as friends. Early European contact indicated that in the old days, the Maori people didn't have any mental illness, but now they are over-represented in the prisons and mental hospitals. This is because doctors don't understand their problems. In Maori communities, if there were problems, the family would come together in the marae and talk it out – even if it took all day. Every person would stand up and let the offender know what they thought, and how that person's behaviour was affecting everyone else. By the end of the day, they would let you know what to do to make yourself acceptable again. They would never let you go away feeling bad. But once European life took over, these systems weakened.

In therapy at The Family Centre, the message we give must be about the pattern – how we can see that they can live again in harmony. It is a message about not being discouraged – how you can get up again when you fall. It must be a message of hope, because when you're down there can still be a lot of hope.

11.

Pura Pura Tuku Iho
(the seed that has been passed down)

by

Flora Tuhaka

This paper describes a presentation that Flora
Tuhaka gave at the 'Just Therapy' conference held in
Duncan, B.C. Canada, in November 1991. In this
presentation, Flora demonstrated how she works
with Maori families who seek her help. For Maori
people an important belief is that one must look into
the past in order to see into the future. Flora's
approach links families deeply into their own
cultural values so that they may find a way forward
out of their difficulties.

This description of Flora's presentation was
written by Carmel Tapping.

Flora began her presentation by explaining a Maori way of life where people lived off the land and took only what was needed from the sea. She spoke of how people hunted, planted and gathered, sharing all their resources with their extended *whanau* (family) and all those who lived around them. Respect was always given to the gods, she said, and the first fish caught and the first fruit or vegetable gathered was given back to the gods in return for a better harvest the following year.

She explained how Maori people were skilled in understanding the natural environment around them; the sun, stars, moon, and the plants and animals. Men and women had their own roles to play and there was a strong sense of community with everyone sharing together, treating each other with kindness and *aroha* (a deep sense of love).

Flora then described the process of urbanisation in the late 1950s and early 1960s, where Maori people were discouraged from building on their own land, and were given government loans for housing in the cities. In these times, cities had plenty of well-paid labouring jobs. She described that, in moving to the cities, the lifestyles of many Maori changed dramatically with much of the traditional ways of living disappearing.

She described how people left the land they owned, the clean plentiful familiar environment that surrounded them, the home of their ancestors. They went to cities where they understood they would be better off.

Maori families were no longer free and easy. They now faced having to pay the cost of their move into the city, paying a home mortgage, higher rates, electricity bills, bus fares to and from work, and having to buy food and clothing. They also had to cope with the everyday difficulties of living in the city. They were not told that everything would cost them money. Many of these families found themselves alone, and were not able to share anymore. As well as being lonely, they experienced the stress of living in an environment that was so foreign to them. It is in this context that many families came for help.

Flora then explained how she works with Maori families. Firstly, it is important that the family understands who they are and where they come from, since these connections are essential elements to the healing process.

When families come to therapy they are greeted in the traditional Maori way. Time is taken to make tribal connections and make links between *whanau* (family) and their extended *whanau*. She then connects herself to the *whanau* through her extended *whanau.* She then becomes a part of them and they a part of her, according to their *whakapapa* (genealogy). She is then discussing as family rather than as client and therapist.

She explained how Maori people, when looking into their lives, look into their past in order to view their future. They must always look behind to see what's in front, which is quite different from the European approach in New Zealand. Maori look to their *tipuna* (ancestors) for wisdom and evidence for the future. In therapy, the process is the same. Families need to let out the pain of the past, so that they can look with hope to their future.

It is important that the family feels comfortable with the worker at an early stage, as this helps draw out the core of their pain and provides a safe atmosphere for the family to share their story. It is important that the family's *wairua* (spiritual soul) flows freely, as this helps people to tell their stories of pain with confidence that the whole family will be treated with respect.

The *wairua* is living and adapts with time to both physical and social needs. The presence of the *wairua* is recognised in all aspects of Maoridom; behind, in front, beside, on top of the *mauri* (life principle) of their heritage. The *wairua* is inherited from birth and is a difficult concept to explain or teach.

When working with Maori families, it is also important that the *mana* (self-respect/status) of any one person is not lowered too quickly. If the *mana* of one is lowered, the *mana* of the whole family is lowered. If a member of the family has been abusive or irresponsible, care needs to be taken not to shame the whole family while the person is challenged or the family will all resist the work. In a European situation, she observed, you can lower the *mana* of an individual, if they are doing something destructive, without necessarily upsetting the rest of the family, since Europeans are held to be individually responsible, unlike Maori, who share responsibility collectively.

Flora presented some examples of her work, including some video footage of therapy sessions with a family who had given permission for this to be shown, and for extracts to appear here. The father in this family had experienced a very difficult and often abusive upbringing. He had spent most of his adult life inside prisons. On occasions he had been very violent, and had been referred to The Family Centre with his family on this occasion because he had attacked his one-year-old daughter. The mother was very depressed and felt hopeless. The father was eventually imprisoned for this offence.

Many of the points Flora had made earlier were illustrated in her interview with the family. At the end of the interview, she offered a reflection that was deeply imbedded in the values of her own and the family's culture:

We would like to thank you for being so open and honest with us. You had the courage to tell us about some bad and terrible things, and that takes a lot of guts.

Charles, you've obviously made some real efforts to change your rough ways, and you've come a long way. You don't hit like you used to, and you admit your faults now, but, there are still some big problems. For example, even this year you've been firing up with Angela and slapping her around, and you abused Frances by calling her dumb, stupid, and saying to her 'you don't know nothing'. Charles, we would like you to think of your uncle, and other Maori men who have disciplined their lives under pressure. We are thinking of those men who lead the haka (traditional dance usually performed by men on special occasions) *or* kaia (leader) *of the* haka. *The strong men who have control over their spontaneous feelings. Years of discipline have taught them* not *to act when they fire up, but to be cool and take time to think. It gets easier with time. You can model on those men. As Maori we know that* women and children are sacred. *We women give birth to the children and the children give life to (our people) the* iwi, *they must never be violated. If we don't treat the women and children like the sacred greenstone, then life is worthless like you have experienced, and we know you don't want that for your family.*

Frances, we know that you know these things. You made it clear that if Charles ever hit you, that would be the finish. We know this is because women are sacred in Maoridom. We also know that you know that children are sacred. That is why you hurt so much when you have to leave Angela at your sister's. We realise it is difficult for you both at the moment, but we are very impressed with how hard you are trying. We reckon good things will happen if you keep at it.

The reflection was a very moving one because it affirmed a way forward for the family, without denying the violence that had occurred Furthermore, the images of *haka,* greenstone (the treasured jewel of Maori), and the sacredness of women and children are all well recognised by Maori people. The reflection linked the family deeply into their own cultural values.

After two interviews, significant changes had occurred. Charles had taken on many of the domestic tasks in the household while he was still unemployed.

Frances had begun to feel confident again. The following are two extracts taken from the reflection after the third interview.

Charles, you're treating your children and Frances as though they are sacred. You clean for them, you wash for them, and you cook for them. They are shining like the shimmering greenstone

Frances does not *tell you to piss off now. She lets you kiss her. We can see that there is more love.*

Flora developed the images in this down-to-earth manner, using the language of the family. It was clear that he was changing and they were moving closer together. At the time of the workshop, the Department of Social Welfare still insisted that the child should not be allowed to return to the family However, since then, Charles has completed his prison sentence, regularly attended the 'Men for Non-Violence' group, and the family has continued with Flora in therapy. The department has now agreed to the child coming home.

After offering these examples of her work with Maori families, Flora ended her presentation with the words: *He rau aroha tuku iho. No reira, ma te Atua koutou katoa e manaaki.* (A precious leaf of knowledge passed down for generations to come. May God bless you all.)

Samoan ways

12.

Honouring Samoan ways and understandings:
Towards culturally appropriate mental health services

by

Kiwi Tamasese

For many years, we have been working here in New Zealand with Samoan families who have migrated to this country. Many of the people who have consulted us have been suffering from what we would call 'immigration trauma' and yet have been diagnosed with any number of psychiatric conditions particularly various forms of psychosis. In receiving referrals from many places, including psychiatric hospitals, Samoan families have come to us bringing with them their medical files and diagnoses. Sometimes these families have also been accompanied by their psychiatrist and we have all talked together about these families' experiences. Over time, it became clear that many of the psychiatrists' conceptions of what was occurring for these families were radically different from the conceptions of the families themselves. It was apparent that these families' perspectives of life, in particular their Samoan cultural beliefs, were in no way fitting with the beliefs of the psychiatric system. It was also clear that these families were being routinely traumatised by the process.

In response to this, we started wondering about how we could bring to light these families' *own* beliefs around mental health, how these knowledges and skills could inform the psychiatric services, and how they could contribute to a policy of different service provision. We decided to conduct a research project about this so that when we spoke about these issues we would not be able to be dismissed as simply telling anecdotes. We applied to the Health Research Council, which is a large health research funding body in New Zealand, and after developing a methodology that everyone was happy with, we were granted research funds.

Three of the key questions we were asking included:

- What are the experiences of Samoan people of the New Zealand mental health system?

- How do Samoan people define mental health?

- What would mental health provision look like if it was based upon Samoan understandings?

The research also explored causes of mental unwellness among Samoan people both generally and in New Zealand, and asked participants to respond to current Pacific Island mental health data.

Responsibilities as researchers

The process of doing the research brought considerable challenges. When we first met with a group of elders to discuss the project they spoke very honestly with us. They said:

Do you realise the significance of what you are asking us to speak about? To speak about what you call conceptions of mental health, involves exposing all that we believe about life and about persons, about selves, about spirit. This kind of knowledge, in our culture, is not public knowledge. It is not to be shared openly with young people (non-elders) like yourselves, because we do not know how you'll handle this type of knowledge. You are asking us to articulate ourselves in relation to our world of spirituality. In matters like this we take great care. There are only particular people who speak about these things and particular places and times when these sorts of conversations take place.

Within the Samoan worldview, great care is taken to ensure that relationships between people, villages, the land and the spirit world remain in good order. When these relationships are disrespected, or crossed in culturally inappropriate ways, there are serious repercussions. What we began to learn from the very beginning of the research process was the responsibility that was expected of us as young people (non-elders) to transmit the knowledge that was shared with us in a form that would keep it safe. This safety involved ensuring that the ways we presented the knowledge stayed as true to it as possible, but also that what was shared would end up being helpful not only for our people but for other people as well. The entire research was therefore shaped by considerations of how to be respectful to the participants and their own knowledges, and also how to create a process that would ensure the guardianship of that knowledge so that it was not misused in any way.

This responsibility weighed heavily upon us particularly because some of the cultural knowledge discussed during the research process had never before been written down, nor had it been passed from one generation to another in the ways that occurred in this project. Samoan culture is organised around genealogical lines and pieces of knowledge are passed through these lines in particular ways. To document the knowledge and make it more widely available was an enormous responsibility. We have an ongoing responsibility to ensure that the participants and their own genealogical lines have access to the report. It contains knowledge that belongs to the participants and also their children, their grandchildren and their grandchildren's grandchildren. Now that we have written the report, we cannot assume that the process has finished. We must instead keep trying to push for the changes to mental health services, the need for which was the whole reason for the research in the first place.

The research methodology

These responsibilities meant that we needed to take great care with the research methodology. So much so, that the methodology actually became a part of the study. When research methods which hold values intrinsic to western cultures are applied to non-western communities, this contributes directly to exclusion. The research we were interested in doing was culturally-based and all those working on it did so under the direction of the Pacific Island Unit of The Family Centre.

We decided to hold a series of focus group interviews with four different groups. There was a group of elder men, a group of elder women, a group of women service providers and a group of men service providers – people who work in mental health services. These group discussions were facilitated by Samoan researchers. We believed that this approach to the research would be an appropriate way of talking among Samoan people as it would allow room for considered opinion, for collective decision making, and significant discussion. We believed that it was appropriate for the participants to be grouped both in terms of gender and by relative status within the cultural community.

Fa'afaletui the weaving of meaning

What evolved from the research was a methodology called *Fa'afaletui* – which is a concept brought to our attention by the Elder Men and Elder Women focus group participants. *Fa'afaletui* describes a process which facilitates the gathering and critical validation of Samoan culture. Each focus group was seen by participants to represent a 'house' or fale. Within these 'houses' of the Elder Men, Elder Women, Women Service Providers and Men Service Providers, information and knowledge were shared and discussed in ways that generated consensus. Within Samoan culture, it is then customary for delegations from each of the 'houses' to meet each other, and to undergo a similar process of consensus-generating discussion. The stories and information from each of the relational 'houses' are threaded and re-threaded between the delegates until all are agreed that the specified knowledge pieces are valid, and represent the collective experience.

Fa'afaletui, then, is the critical process of weaving (tui) together all the different threads of knowledge from the different 'houses'. The culmination of this process is a collective representation that substantially enhances the Samoan world view.

Language

Before describing what emerged from the discussion with the different focus groups, it seems important to talk a little about the importance of language itself. Samoan traditions of knowledge and history are communicated by what is known as oral tradition, a tradition that is often minimised by Western writers and seen as somehow 'less than' written traditions. However, what is rarely addressed within these Western critiques is that Samoan traditions, and other indigenous traditions, are 'written' into geographical sites and locations, familial names, honorifics and titles, genealogy, ritual and chant. Oral tradition, as such, is not a haphazard or indiscriminate espousing of information, but the transmission of cultural information and knowledge (knowledge that is critical to belonging and identity) which has undergone its own process of validation, synthesis and analysis.

A primary function of language is to be a vehicle which communicates the ways in which individuals and collectives of people perceive, interact, and respond to the world in which they live. Within language, the underlying values, norms, mores, indeed the belief systems of that culture are transmitted. For all people, the language which best interprets and explains the realities of their world view can be said to be their first language, their language of identity and belonging. This language can be said to be their first paradigm, the social construct which houses and maintains their identity and which gives meaning to their lives.

The Samoan language, depending upon the situation, is spoken either in informal ways, or in a mode that is highly formal. The latter is the language of ritual, the language through which knowledge is appropriately and most often imparted. When speaking in this formal language, the presence of protocol and etiquette is most keenly felt. This etiquette involves not only words spoken but also body language. More often that not, it is body language which gives context and meaning to the message. For example, a person offering an apology while maintaining direct eye contact with the offended party, will not be taken seriously.

In order to undertake research with Samoan speaking participants, the intricacies of Samoan language need to be understood. As researchers we needed to be fluent in Samoan. We also needed to be able to understand what was being conveyed in the context of the Samoan worldview. We also had to be able to respond to that worldview. And finally, we needed to find ways to bridge the two worldviews (Samoan and English) without compromising the first paradigm.

A Samoan report and an English report

Bridging the two worldviews offered us many challenges. As the focus group interviews were conducted in the Samoan language we were immediately faced with the issue of translation. At first, what we did was transcribed and translated the focus group conversations into English. This was a job that involved some 350 pages of translation. We had hoped to analyse these conversations, to articulate the themes that emerged in them, by using the English translations. But it gradually became clear that there was something wrong with this process. The more we translated, the more it altered the meaning of what had actually been said. I remember one weekend I was reading through the translations of the transcripts, and came across an example where the meaning had been significantly altered in relation to knowledge that would be considered in Samoan culture to be sacred. I realised that what we were doing was really dangerous – although it is standard researching practice. And so we called a halt to the whole process, and re-thought everything.

We turned back to original Samoan transcripts, and decided to work from these. We stepped into the language that had been used in the focus groups. We then began to cluster words and phrases until we developed themes that represented the key knowledges that had been expressed. Finally, we wrote the report in Samoan. Copies of the draft report were given to authoritative participant members from each of the groups to check for coherency, appropriate language use and an appropriate observance of written protocols and etiquette. After this process we then translated the key concepts of the Samoan report into English. In this way, two reports were created from this research, one in Samoan and one in English. This process has changed our views about some key aspects of research. As researchers, we now consider that translating knowledge from one language to another and doing the analysis in this second language is a suspect methodological process.

Some of the findings from the research

It is not possible to convey here all the findings that were derived from this research project. The rest of this paper focuses on some of the key differences between Samoan understandings of self and Western conceptions as these differences have profound implications in terms of responding to mental health issues. [For a summary of some of the other key findings of this research it is possible to obtain the full research report from The Family Centre.]

Samoan understandings of self
In the process of the research, it became clear that Samoan descriptions of the meaning of self vary greatly from western conceptions.

The self as relational
The description of persons or selves in a Samoan context is that the person exists in relationship to other people both living and those who have passed on:

> *I cannot say that I am a person, just me... I am nothing without my other connections.* (Service Provider Men)

> *The self is identity* [fa'asinomaga] *and tofi* [responsibilities, heritage and duties]. (Service Provider Women)

> *The idea that a person can be an individual unto him/herself is a new concept which was introduced by Christianity ...* (Service Provider Men)

The participants in the research articulated how, as Samoans, their identities exist in relation to others from specific locations of belonging such as their villages, districts and country. What's more, they are born into genealogical continuums and during their lifetimes undertake positions and roles of responsibility in relation to these genealogies. The participants established that the relational Samoan self is legitimised by identity and belonging, genealogy and roles, responsibility and heritage.

This sense of personhood is not generationally bound – for instance, one's personhood is still defined in relation to one's great great great grandmother. Samoan persons understand that they are the embodiment of all those relationships that have gone on, both good and bad, before them. Because the self is described in these ways, it acts as an impediment for people to behave inappropriately in case generations that come after them will carry the shame of their own actions. But likewise, the good deeds of the past generations are carried by the present generation.

These relationships, which are central to Samoan identity, are considered to be sacred and there are rituals of protocol and etiquette designed to protect them. This sense of the sacred, of spirituality, informs every aspect of Samoan life.

Relations to land and sea

Samoan descriptions of self are in relationship not only to past and future generations and to each other now in the present, but also to the land, the forests and the sea. Samoans born in Samoa, are born to families who are a part of extended relations, who each have a part of the land of their village which is seen to be connected to them. Their identity is linked to this land. When you ask someone where they are from, they will speak of their identity as being tied to a piece of land, a piece of the sea, a part of the forest from the village of their past relations. They may not be linked as strongly to the place where they are currently living.

This connection to land, sea and forest is again linked to spirituality. In the Samoan worldview there are important connections between the Gods, the physical environment of land and sea, and the Samoan people. Genealogy can be said to exist within a theological context. The term *fa'asinomaga* relates to those places which locate the Samoan person within the spiritual, physical, and historical continuums of Samoan identity and belonging.

In these ways the Samoan person is seen to both physical and spiritual in nature – in fact there is no separation of these concepts. When we talk about mental health, it is not seen as a separate category of health. It is a part of the total health and well-being of people, land and sea.

Harmony as metaphor for mental health

This means that the key metaphors associated with mental health in a Samoan context are in great contrast to those of Western cultures. The principle quest of Samoan people is to seek harmony. People seek harmony in relationship with God/s. They seek harmony in relationship with each other, and they seek harmony in relationship with their environment. A range of daily protocols and ways of living seek to protect and re-generate harmony in these relationships. Mental ill-health is understood to result from disharmony.

Two key metaphors associated with mental well-being include '*tupuaga*' and '*tofiga*':

Tupuaga literally means – that which we have arisen from, that which we have grown out of. The metaphor is one of growing out of the soil, growing out of a piece of ground. Where other cultures have primary metaphors around birthing, this Samoan metaphor evokes growing out of rich genealogical traditions.

Tofiga refers to that which has been given to you to be responsible for. These responsibilities include family relationships, relationships with the land, responsibilities in terms of maintaining health, and also responsibilities in terms of addressing any ill that people do to each other. *Tofiga* is also a metaphor about responsibility to language and to rituals. These are responsibilities, not only towards the past, but primarily to the future. The present generation has a responsibility for the children of the future.

Mental ill-health among Samoan people is often understood as being the result of breaches of *Tofiga* and/or some disruption of *Tupuaga*.

These are some of the key metaphors that inform Samoan perspectives of life and health and they have significant implications in terms of responding to crises of mental health.

Implications of the Samoan worldview meeting the western worldview

When the Samoan worldview meets with Western metaphors of mental health, they couldn't be more different and this has serious implications. Western science upholds a mind/body split and an individualistic conception of the self that is profoundly different from Samoan perspectives. Western medicine and the health professions are based on assumptions about the self that are rarely questioned and that are simply assumed to be the only ways of understanding life and health. What this often means is that when Samoan families in New Zealand are referred to mental health services in a crisis they can become more crazy rather than less. They find themselves in a situation in which there are two descriptions of reality, two descriptions of the self, which are in conflict with one another.

Within psychiatric services, the Western description of self has the upper hand and the Samoan families are treated accordingly. If the Samoan family tells the doctor about their alternative description of the problem – that they believe the symptoms being displayed could be due to a break in relationships with other people (living or no longer living), to breaches in protocol and etiquette, or to dislocation from land and a sense of belonging – they are likely to be dismissed and this dismissal can contribute to the person concerned becoming more crazy. What's more, the Samoan families' faith in their own belief system may be eroded and their cultural descriptions of life may become subjugated.

In such a process, the mental health service never acts alone. Its cultural descriptions are confirmed by the wider New Zealand society, including the church. There is considerable support for the view that the spiritual world and the physical world are separate, that the person is simply individually sick, and indeed that there is probably something wrong with their personality, or their brain, or some other psychological aspect. If the Samoan family is interested in talking about what a particular ancestor might have done to contribute to the current situation, if they are speculating that there must have been some break in protocol or ritual, then the doctors are likely to see this as further pathology, and certain forms of Christianity are likely to disparage these views as pagan beliefs.

The participants in the research were clear about the debilitating effects that these processes have on Samoan families. They were also clear about the alternatives.

Where to from here?

When describing their conceptions of a successful mental health service for Samoan people, all the participants in the research referred to hospital and community based services designed and largely staffed by Samoan people. They clearly named a service where the Samoan conceptions of self or persona would be the basis of any mental health service provision. Addressing key cultural factors such as the relational arrangements, including expected roles and responsibilities, would have a central place in the service delivery.

Our main hope for this research is to invite mental health services to include not only the psychiatric / Western understanding of the self as the basis of their interventions, but when working with Samoan families to engage with, and indeed base their understandings around, Samoan conceptions of the self.

Mental health services for Samoan families need to be underpinned by Samoan conceptions of self, health and personhood. We certainly believe that certain aspects of western psychiatric understandings have a function within these services, but it is a limited function. Services need to be informed by the cultural understandings of the populations which they are designed to serve.

If mental health services acknowledged multiple descriptions of self and identity, then service provision would look significantly different. It is possible to imagine services including Samoan people who are psychiatrists trained in clinical Western ways, while also incorporating appropriate Samoan people (traditional healers) who have specialised roles and knowledges about mental ill health in Samoan culture. In this way, services would not be solely medically bound. Medicine would continue to help contain some of the symptomology of mental health crises (participants in the research acknowledged that this can be very important), while culturally appropriate responses to Samoan people in relation to mental ill health could also be developed.

Structural changes

It will require significant structural changes to enable some of the most vulnerable people in our society to have the possibility of receiving mental health services on their own terms in ways that address their concepts of self and their relational understandings of life. For too long health professionals have been doing the best they can to 'treat' members of different cultures with inadequate knowledge of those cultures and with western understandings that are incompatible with the understandings of those they are working with.

The fundamental issues are structural issues. How can space be made for other conceptions of the self and mental health to be put forward? How can the capacity within communities such as the Samoan community be built so that they can develop what we call in New Zealand their own 'provider services' run according to their own world views? It is not necessarily going to be the case that these communities will want to run everything themselves, but it will be critical that they have significant control of the direction of these services through well formed partnerships. How can resources be re-orientated so that members of the Samoan community, and other cultural communities, receive their proportion of tax-payer dollars spent on mental health services on their own terms? We have a long way to go to answer these questions, but at least they are now being asked.

Further challenges

These research findings bring further challenges. If notions of self, identity and health are intricately intertwined with issues of land and spirituality then this challenges health professionals to engage with the broader struggles associated with land, language and identity. It becomes important work to engage with the issue of land reform. It also becomes important work to engage with the issue of the reclamation of language. These findings invite therapists, community workers and researchers to move beyond what has been seen as their current domain of action. They invite considerations of *tofiga* – a sense of broader cultural responsibility. They invite considerations of responsibilities to each other, to those who are no longer alive, and to those who are yet to be born.

Other key findings of the research

Other key findings of the research involved the pressures placed on Samoan families in New Zealand and the effectiveness of current mental health services for Samoan families. What follows are summaries of the findings in these two areas.

Pressures on Samoan families in New Zealand

The research found that for Samoan families in New Zealand there are a range of additional pressures which contribute to mental ill-health. A number of themes were documented including:

- The absence of the interaction between extended families and communities of people weakens relational arrangements.

- The values of the dominant culture contribute to excluding Samoan ways of being and living.

- Financial pressures result in feelings of failure, isolation and fear.

- Lack of access to traditional means of healing and restoring relationships means that families delay seeking help and have few options as to where to turn.

Effectiveness of current services

Participants were disturbed by the summary of Pacific Island Mental Health data that was presented to them. They were particularly worried about the growing numbers of Pacific Island clients being treated in the mental health area. Concern was expressed about the discriminatory aspects of a monocultural western system for Samoan peoples. Concern was also consistently expressed about their perceptions of the use of sedation as a treatment rather than a form of containment. Language was also identified as a barrier to appropriate treatment.

The current services were seen to be effective where the problems were largely physical or where provision of care for the mentally ill in hospitals lighten the load for families and enable some family members to take on full time employment and/or other tasks. The recent employment of cultural consultants and advisors was viewed as an exciting indication of new possibilities in the mental health system that are in their infancy, but which were seen to possess the seeds of hope.

13.

Multiple sites of healing:
Developing culturally appropriate responses

by

Kiwi Tamasese

Here at The Family Centre, over many years we have responded to Samoan families in situations where a member has been admitted to a psychiatric hospital. By acknowledging the multiple sites of identity that inform the Samoan world view, we approach our work with Samoan families with an openness to multiple sites of healing. If the Samoan understanding of self exists in relationship to other people, to land, sea and forests, to the Gods, to the ancestors and so on, then all of these relationships can be sites for significant healing.

If it is believed that mental ill health is due to a disruption to relationships with people who are present and alive, then the work we are involved in is to re-establish those relationships. If the disjuncture is in relationship to land then we are involved in reconnecting people with their lands. If the disjuncture is with ancestors, or with the Gods then this is one place where healing can take place. While we can only help so much with this, we will call in appropriate people from the community to be involved in the processes that will be required.

The first step in creating culturally appropriate responses to mental ill-health is to make it possible for the family to be able to talk about what they believe is occurring. We take care so that people will feel free to tell us what they think is really going on. We try to ensure that they know that we are not interested in imposing upon them any descriptions of life / health / self that we might have, and that we wish to hear from them their understandings, according to their own frames of meaning. If the family is believing that something very frightening is taking place then we must take great care with this. We try to provide the spiritual safety for them to talk about that which is most frightening.

An example of a situation that requires extreme care is when a family might believe that it is suffering from the effects of a curse. In such a situation, we don't try to reconstruct and enforce upon the family an alternative meaning from the outside. Instead, we are interested in providing a context in which they can talk about and explore these frightening things. If, within the course of conversation, someone mentions their grandmother who has died, we might say something like, 'Shall we take some steps to protect this conversation? Shall we say some prayers together before we talk some more about this.' By taking these steps we are honouring the significance of the conversation and are making it possible for the family to share their beliefs with us. This process is not without dilemmas. We are very conscious that if we are creating a context for prayer then we must take care not to imply a particular version of a Christian worldview that would imply that the family had 'sinned' in some way. Instead, we are concerned with creating a spiritually safe context for people to talk about their experiences in ways that are congruent with their cultural traditions, and we are trying to ensure that we are not imposing any form of outside interpretation upon what they are going through. In our experience, taking this sort of care makes a big difference to families at a time of crisis.

We use particular words to signal to the family that we are willing to engage with their beliefs and worldview and that we are not frightened. We might say something like, 'You have mentioned to us these experiences with your grandmother and, if you feel safe to do so, we can help you talk about these. But there are also other people in our culture who could help you and us to find peace with grandma again, to seek her forgiveness. We cannot do this. We are too young and we are not of the right status. We are not from the village from where you come. But we know some people, some elders who may be able to help, if you would like this to happen.'

Invariably the family will take us up on this invitation and together we begin planning a ritual that will make a difference. We talk with the family about material things that may be needed for the ritual, and we also talk about spiritual, emotional and mental preparations that will need to take place. This becomes a focus for conversations and for different family members to play different roles. These cultural processes provide a context for conversations and they honour the significance of what is occurring. This process also provides the opportunity to call upon people in the community who are greatly respected and who have considerable experience in addressing crises. Many people become involved in what are collective processes of healing and the restoration of relationships. It is not possible to convey here the intricacies of these rituals and community processes, except to say that these rituals can play a significant part in the healing process for Samoan families.

In every culture there are healing traditions. We are interested in engaging with these to create culturally appropriate responses to families in crisis. Just as in the Samoan worldview there are multiple sites of identity, we are interested in working with multiple sites of healing. Rituals and ceremony might have a part to play in some circumstances, as might reconnection to land, family meetings, conversations with an elder and so on (even western medicine may have a role to play in responding to symptoms of mental ill health). What we are interested in doing is honouring the cultural meanings and understandings of the families who are seeking our assistance and responding appropriately and respectfully.

Matters of gender

14.

Gender and culture – together

by

Kiwi Tamasese

As women from subjugated cultures we have tried to point out that it is not helpful to us when gender and culture are talked about in ways that imply they exist separately and independently of one another. It is also misleading. The ways in which 'gender' and 'culture' are sometimes talked about seems to lift both these concepts out of relationship. In some conversations it seems as if gender is in some way separate from the general ways in which people live their lives, as if gender resides within individuals. Similarly, the ways in which 'culture' is sometimes spoken about makes it sound as if it is a fixed entity. This is especially true when people speak about 'true culture' – as if the only true culture is that elusive entity that existed pre-colonisation. These constructions of gender and of culture are problematic, particularly for women from subjugated cultures who wish to address issues of gender. If our gender and our culture are constructed as somehow separate from each other, as soon as we attempt to take any action in relation to either issues of gender or culture, we find our identities called into question. For instance, when I return to Samoa with other Samoan women we must take great care to ensure that we are not perceived as white feminists. However, back in New Zealand, in trying to ensure that issues of culture are considered in all projects, white feminist women may believe that we are 'privileging culture over gender'.

Gender and culture cannot be separated. Our ways of living as women and as men are always influenced by the symbols, rituals, language and relationship structures of culture. Recognising that gender cannot be separated from culture does not mean that we are privileging culture *over* gender. It means that whenever we are talking about gender, cultural considerations are relevant, as are other considerations of class and sexuality etc. Similarly, wherever we are talking about culture, relations of gender are relevant.

We have tried to create an alternative way of approaching issues of gender and culture. This is a framework which focuses on the liberative traditions within all cultures. Within all our people's histories there are non-liberative as well as liberative stories, traditions and practices. As we have written about elsewhere, the principles of belonging, liberation and sacredness, and their inter-relationship, inform every aspect of our work. We're interested in playing our part to contribute to the traditions of belonging that are liberative, and that we could call sacred. Many sacred traditions are not liberative – so we do not make these our focus. And some liberative traditions don't emphasise belonging, so similarly we do not concentrate on these. We believe in creating contexts to further those traditions and practices in which belonging, liberation and sacredness meet. And we believe that this is a challenge for all peoples within our own cultures.

What this has meant in terms of issues of gender and culture is that in order to address issues of gender justice we do not need to take an oppositional view of culture. Instead we are interested in tracing the liberative gender arrangements within a particular culture and finding ways that these traditional arrangements can inform our work. Let me describe this process in relation to Samoan culture.

In order to find ways of grounding our current work on issues of gender in history, we thoroughly researched the traditions of gender arrangement within Samoan culture and by doing so unearthed liberative traditions. Specifically, our analysis of pre-colonised Samoa revealed a covenant relationships (feagaiga) between brother and sister that had the capacity to equalise the relationships between women and men. We learnt of traditional gender arrangements of partnership, and of the positions of respect that women had been held within Samoan culture. This research was an involved process that we took very seriously. The fact that we can identify traditions within the culture that promote the sorts of gender relations to which we aspire has made our work in the present considerably easier. It has gone on to inform a range of projects within the Samoan community on issues of gender and culture that do not bring the two into opposition (Tamasese 1998). And it has meant that as Samoan women we have been able to work on issues of gender without having our cultural identity questioned.

Elsewhere we have written about the ways in which we have developed partnerships across issues of culture and gender within the Family Centre (see Tamasese & Waldegrave 1996; Tamasese, Waldegrave, Tuhaka & Campbell 1998) and so I won't go into this in any detail here. These are partnerships that are based on values of humility, respect, sacredness, reciprocity and love. They are also based on structures of accountability through caucusing, and leadership within these caucuses, that seek to protect against gender and culture bias in our day-to-day work. The Maori and Pacific island sections are self-determining, while the Pakeha (white section) runs its own affairs but is accountable to the other two sections. Similarly the women and the men caucus separately at times to address their own issues. As with the cultural work, we have found it helpful to agree to creative forms of accountability that address our gendered histories and consequent biases. The women's work is self-determining. The men manage their own responsibilities but are accountable to the women.

What I will mention here is what these partnerships, these relationships, mean to me. Our partnerships and the structures of these partnerships have meant that we are not constantly locked into an oppositional frame. The partnerships provide space for separate men's and women's discussions, and for separate cultural caucuses. In these separate spaces groups are actively involved in the deconstruction and the reconstruction of gender and cultural traditions. The caucuses are also places where sustenance and support can be found in ways that further the partnerships.

For me to be able to spend my life working on issues of gender and culture requires these long-term relationships. I need the ongoing relationships with men and with people of other cultures at The Family Centre in order to be able to move into the outside world and address issues of culture and of gender. These relationships sustain me. Sometimes there are difficulties but we all know that these are long-term committed relationships to one another. We know that in time the difficulties will be sorted out.

15.

Gender –

The impact of western definitions of womanhood on other cultures

Kiwi Tamasese &
Luamanuvao Winnie Laban

This paper describes presentations given by Kiwi Tamasese and Luamanuvao Winnie Laban, of the Pacific Island Section of The Family Centre, at the 'Just Therapy' conference held in Duncan, B.C. Canada in November 1991. These presentations focused on gender issues, with an emphasis on the impact Western notions of feminism and womanhood have had on Pacific Island women. Their strong message was that no culture can avoid the discussion of the relationship between men and women.

This description of their presentations was written by Carmel Tapping.

Luamanuvao Winnie, in her opening of the discussion on gender and culture, called on the women and men present to 'look into your own stories and you will find healing'. It was a poignant moment, as the invitation for people whose cultures had undergone colonisation to remember their own stories is an invitation into pain. Systematic destruction of culture and language, the forced settling of lands, the diseases that killed many, the massacres, the destruction of cultural values, and the imposing of structures, rituals and, more specifically, the gender arrangements of colonising cultures, are all painful issues.

The effects of this history – homelessness, alcoholism, under-achievement in education, unemployment, and continual marginalisation through present-day government policies – result in daily lives of pain. The high incidence of violence in the home is a measure of the internalised violation which indigenous peoples have experienced in many countries throughout the years. Albert Wendt in *Ola* states the totality of this pain: *I know, yes, this person knows, that he is what he has lost.*

The pain is formidable, the losses immense. That response to Luamanuvao's invitation can be reluctant is understandable. Yet in entering into their stories: *We are reminded of our courage, and that, despite the systematic decimations, we have survived. The pain has not finally broken us, neither women nor men.*

Luamanuvao Winnie recalled her own woman's story (Falenaoti 1992). Before the missionaries' arrival, the primary familial relationship hi her own culture was between brother and sister. The sister, when born, is known as Tamasa or sacred child, and the brother, tama tane or male child. The relationship between the two is a covenant, in her language, *feagaiga.* The covenant relationship ensures the sister's powers of blessing and cursing. In this arrangement, brothers were required to seek their sister's agreement for any decisions relating to land or titles. Without that agreement he risked a curse which could become intergenerational. Likewise, brothers and their families were blessed when they kept to the sacred covenant relationship.

This provided an authentic structural balance between the genders in Samoan society.

However, the advent of the missionaries in her own country, beginning in the 1930s, declared this gender arrangement to be pagan: *Only God can bless or curse,* they said. The destruction of the covenant relationship between brother and sister began the demise of Samoa's own gender arrangement at familial, village, district and national level.

The scripting of Samoan womanhood into images of Eve (the suffering temptress who is mother of all) and Mary (the pure virgin), fulfilled the conditions of the patriarchal gender system which characterised Christianity. This imposition on Samoa's own gender arrangement left her own people vulnerable to the gender definitions of the patriarchal structures embodied in the government administration and the cash economy. The three claws of colonisation – religion, administration, and cash economy – have their roots in Western patriarchal values.

While European religion and education have had major influences on Samoan traditional gender arrangements, memories and fragments of the covenant relationship still remain with her people. Thus Winnie's invitation for us to recover our cultural memories is pertinent. She stated that, as indigenous peoples, they are relegated to the periphery for survival. As women who daily live out the violent prescriptions of patriarchy, they need their own cultural anchors to light the way to liberating gender arrangements. Their daily struggle is to remember their own stories of manhood, of womanhood, and the gender arrangements which sustained them in the past.

Look into your own stories and you will find healing

Winnie pointed out that all our cultures have stories of womanhood and manhood. All our cultures have their own gender arrangements. But, as Waldegrave (1990) points out:

Men, almost entirely, have developed and controlled our modern market-orientated economies. For over two centuries they negotiated a path through scientific research, industrial invention, colonial enterprise (including the slave trade), industrial development, capital expansion, and post-industrial technology. They took control of public life, defining it for themselves, and assigned the private family sphere to women. This division of labour, driven by pervasive economic forces and patriarchal logic, soon became institutionalised. Exceptions to it arose during times of short labour supply, as for example in wartime.

Each colonial administration either subjugated or rescripted the gender arrangements of the colonised. The vertical gender arrangement characteristic of the colonists was the frame into which many people were forced. The resultant loss of status and power by women of many colonised cultures is mistakenly attributed to their traditional customs and, in this respect, the tendency of colonists to apportion blame to the colonised is clearly apparent.

The influences of dominant cultures and their prescribed gender arrangements are just as strong today. The media and their promotion of certain images of womanhood and manhood of the dominant culture raise expectations and initiate dreams.

The prevailing notions of womanhood and manhood in the dominant culture define lives for women and men of marginalised cultures. The power differences between the two genders in the dominant culture become a reality also for the marginalised. Western feminism, with its limited critique of cultural, class and religious difference amongst women, exacerbates this problem. The universalising of the analyses of patriarchy as practised by many European and North American white women, denies the different stories in other cultures.

An analysis of the Samoan story clearly indicates that it was colonisation which introduced the patriarchy of modernity. Now we all share that patriarchy, but our analysis and our solutions for the future draw on different traditions. *We draw on the liberative traditions in our culture.* In our case, the covenant tradition is central. As Audre Lorde says:

> *To imply, however, that all women suffer the same oppression simply because we are women is to lose sight of the many varied tools of patriarchy. It is to ignore how those tools are used by women, without awareness, against each other.*

Kiwi Tamasese revealed that Samoan women continue to survive double deprivation in New Zealand. They are deprived because they are women, and deprived because they are Samoans. Economic survival for many Pacific Island families in New Zealand has meant mothers taking on two or even three lowly-paid menial jobs – commonly as night-shift cleaners in office buildings, and existing on only a few hours' sleep each day while also caring for their families:

Lack of statistical data on Pacific Island women is a loud statement of the disregard for our reality here in New Zealand: a reality usually lived through in silence; a reality of low-paid menial jobs; a reality of having to supplement the family income while also having to look after our children; a reality that, after doing the best we can, our children end up like us in menial jobs. We are the budgeters supreme; we are the organisers of many a community group; we are often your unpaid volunteers upholding your social equality myth. We have been pained by your dual forces of sexism and racism, yet we are undaunted, for in us is the richness of our cultural heritages that New Zealand badly needs. We are survivors and our children will survive. (Tamasese, Masoe-Clifford & Ne'emia-Garwood 1988)*

Kiwi's observation that Pacific Island women have been pained by the dual forces of sexism and racism is an important one. They live in a dominant white culture, which defines normality within its own meaning system, yet to be a Maori or Samoan demands different attitudes and values. We need to be mindful of the painful distortions they need to practice in order to conform.

McGoldrick et al. (1989) make the point that cultural stereotyping often focuses on the physical characteristics of a group, this being much more problematic for women than men, since women in our society are still valued above all by their appearance. Such pressure to conform results in, for example, Jewish women changing the shape of their noses, black women straightening their hair, and those with dark skin trying to appear lighter. There is also pressure to conform to the Western ideal of unnatural slimness.

These writers acknowledge that since gender arrangements are transmitted through the culture, challenging the sexism of a family involves challenging its culture in a way that could be experienced as extremely threatening. The issue of gender in relation to culture is a very sensitive one, and it is often said that one of the most difficult challenges for family therapy is how to intervene clinically in a way that respects culture while at the same time challenges gender inequities.

Kiwi made the important point, however, that it is only people who belong to a culture who should make decisions about what is, or is not, oppressive or limiting for them. This is not the prerogative of the dominant culture or its therapists. Luamanuvao Winnie Laban stated that every culture must ask who holds the power within that culture, and for what reason.

Luamanuvao Winnie invited women to 'look into your own stories and you will find healing' – that the stories of pain, poverty, hardship and racial oppression must be told. On this theme, Joan Laird (1989) writes of how, until very recently, women's stories have been largely untold and unheard.

> *The history of anthropology, for instance, is a history of men. To learn about the cultures of the world is still, for the most part, to learn the stories of men and of male production. Women have always had their private stories, as both male and female anthropologists are discovering, but until recently we did not know how to listen to them,* (p.428-429)

She relates, too, how women and their lives have been largely unsung, unstoried, unmythologised, while their accomplishments, if noted at all, are recorded hi small and private ways.

> *Whenever men fulfil their duties creditably, they are lauded. In company they tell endless stories about their adventures, for their duties are always 'adventures'; they hold stag feasts of religious importance after a successful hunt. Even the mythology occupies itself with the pursuits and rewards of men. The important visions, which men have been driven all their youth to pursue, bestow power for the masculine occupations. A successful hunter can parade this fact in ways licensed by his visions – songs that he sings publicly, amulets that are conspicuous and worn in public, charms that he can sell. Women's work 'is spoken of neither for good nor evil' – at least in a gathering of men. Conventionally it is not judged in any way, it is simply not given any thought.* (Landes 1971, in Laird 1989, p.438)

She argues that, as therapists, we need to know how to listen to the stories women tell, to search for and respect the ways in which they tell their stories, and to assist them to make choices about the ways they wish to story their futures. Luamanuvao Winnie emphasised that these stories take place in cultural contexts, which provide the space and differentiating aspects of the future stories.

References

Falenaoti, M.T. 1992: 'Slna e Salll.' In press.

Laird, J. 1989: 'Women and stories: restorying women's self-constructions.' In McGoldrick, M., Anderson, C.M. & Walsh, F. (eds): *Women In Families. A framework for family therapy.* New York: W.W.Norton.

Lorde, A. 1984: *Sister Outsider. Essays and speeches by Audre Lorde.* The Crossing Press, Feminist Series.

McGoldrick, M., Garcia-Preto, N., Moore Mines, P. & Lee, E. 1989: 'Ethnicity and women.' In McGoldrick, M., Anderson, C.M. & Walsh, F. (eds): *Women In Families. A framework for family therapy.* New York. W.W.Norton.

Tamasese, K., Masoe-Clifford, P. & Ne'Emia-Garwood, S. 1988: *Pacific Island Peoples' Perspectives.* Report of the Royal Commission on Social Policy, Vol.4.

Waldegrave, C. 1990: 'Social justice & family therapy.' *Dulwich Centre Newsletter, 1.*

Wendt, A. 1991: 'Inside us our dead.' In *Ola.* Penguin.

Working on issues of violence and abuse

16.

Stop Abuse
Project

by

Kiwi Tamasese

On speaking about this project I wish to
acknowledge the Samoan Advisory Council
(Wellington) for their leadership of the project; The
Family Centre for their facilitation of the project; the
trainers for their dedication and hard work in the
project; and all the participants for their will to end
violence in our families and communities.

In 1992 we began a project called 'Stop Abuse' in Wellington, New Zealand. There was an incident in the media in which Jenny Shipley, the now Prime Minister of New Zealand, erroneously made a link between the growth in incidence of child abuse in New Zealand to the growth of Pacific Islander immigration to New Zealand. In this way she implied that the Pacific Island community is abusive and violent. Not surprisingly we took offence at this.

We organised a number of meetings of the Samoan community and invited Jenny Shipley to come along. The community asked her to acknowledge her own mistakes and apologise to the community, and she did this. The community also said that they shared her concerns about addressing violent behaviours. They said, 'You were wrong in stating that there is a predominance of violence in our relationships, but there is violence in some relationships and we want to address this'. As a result, she funded a project called 'Stop Abuse'.

The project started out in ten or twelve locations in the Wellington area. We held separate training for older men and older women, younger men and younger women. The groups would come together at the end of two day periods to share their conversations. In our experience, holding separate gender and age groups has been very important.

For us, as Samoan people, where there is a matter of importance, an issue that touches the whole life of our people, it is important that we discuss it not only as a collective – at the village level – but also that we discuss it in gendered collectives – as a group of women and a group of men. There is a feeling that there are boundaries of discussion between the genders particularly around matters of sexuality. The only way that matters related to sexuality can be talked about in depth is to have separate gender groups. Within the separate groups there is some degree of common experience, there will be differences too, but there will be common ground. The group of women need to come to a consensus on their views of the issue, as do the men. The only way this can be done equitably is through single gender groups. Having separate age groups means that the voices of young women and young men can also be heard and honoured.

Within the 'Stop Abuse' Project all of the groups began by building a sense of belonging and strength to deal with the issue of violence. We then looked at the definition of violence and how it is lived out. We set about establishing a community consensus on what is violent and what is not. By doing this it meant that we had to rely very little on workers' judgements. The community came up with their own definitions of what is violent and what is not. Great care was taken in the ways in which we did this. We called the exercise 'Drawing the Line'.

We asked the members of the community to identify behaviours that they considered to be examples of physical, economic, spiritual, psychological and sexual violence. We asked for five examples of each type of violence. The examples ranged from overt assault to less dramatic examples of harassment.

We then asked the participants to 'draw the line' as to what violence they wanted stopped in the community. A lot of negotiations would then take place as we tried to facilitate a consensus. Importantly within these discussions the final judgement of what behaviour is okay and what is not okay is always decided by those who have suffered from it. We ask people throughout the discussions to put themselves in the places of those who have experienced the particular example of violence. We ask questions like, 'Would the people who experience this think it is okay? If not, why not? Do you still think it is okay?'

This principle of the right for those people who have been subject to violence to determine where the line should be drawn is also structured into the program. At the end of the separate training day sessions the different groups (older men, older women, younger women, younger men) all come together. As a community we then come up with a consensus of where we wish to draw the line. As facilitators we are clear that at the end of the day the 'drawing of the line' needs to satisfy the group that are most hurt by the violence, that are most affected. As sexual abuse is mostly experienced by women and young women, we are clear that where the line is drawn must satisfy the women. What is also important is that, by the end of the exercise, the men must be able to see the importance of this and the reasons behind it.

Having established a community consensus on what is violent behaviour and what is not, we then explore different ways of stopping violence. As most violence is perpetrated by men, we look at ways of ensuring a restitution of the place of respect for women within the family, within organisations, within the churches, and within the culture itself.

One of the direct outcomes of this work was that the community named a Sunday of each year as 'Stop Abuse Sunday'. The community wanted to see a particular Sunday to focus on these issues, and to remember those who have suffered. It is also a day of recommitment to non-violent behaviour. Many of the men who attended the training days continue to work to live lives free of violence, and also to run groups to help other men do likewise.

Another direct result of the Project is that participants have identified that they have come to know more about the gender arrangements that were a part of Samoan culture before the Christian missionaries arrived. This knowledge had dispersed. Participants said they came to learn of the gender arrangements of partnerships, and the positions of respect that women had within Samoan culture. And they reconnected with the culture's deep commitment to its own futures – the children.

17.

Challenges from within the culture

by

Warihi Campbell

For fourteen years I have been working with men who are violent – in the Maori community and in prisons. It was Maori women who first challenged us to look at men's violence. They were challenging to us. Three groups grew from there: the Maori men's group, the Pakeha men's group, and the Samoan men's group. We still have contact. As Maori men, we went out looking at all the men's groups operating at the time but we could find none that were of our culture. We turned to our elders and they said, 'Everything is around you. You didn't need to go anywhere.' Our ancestors are our professors.

And so we have been developing our own ways of working. Our ways are often different than other people's ways. We have different understandings. We understand that when a man hits a partner then he is hitting her ancestors. We understand that, within the Maori community, 'Your children are my children. If you hurt them, you hurt me. We are Maori.'

Our different understandings affect the ways in which we work. As men we speak of our connections to the land and of how we are connected to woman – how we are born from both. We speak of how, if we are able as men to acknowledge mother Earth, then we ought to be able to acknowledge the significance of women – the other side of life. We speak of the importance of challenging men's violence to women because women are the bearers of the next generation. If we break the bearers then we will not have another generation. All these ways of speaking and understanding come from within our culture, and that is so important.

Sometimes I cry when I speak of these topics because I know the hurt of the men. But I know deeper the hurt of the partners they are married to. I have seen them bruised. I've seen them nearly killed. I'll be in this job for as long as my two feet can walk because, as a priest, I do not like to take the body of the partner onto the *marae* [the Maori term for community/spiritual meeting place] when I have had the opportunity to stop the violence. The men I work with know that I do not want them to leave their actions on my conscience. As an elder, they know the significance of this. They know that challenging from within our culture will continue.

He Whakatau, Faafetai and Acknowledgement

Charles Waldegrave, Kiwi Tamasese, Flora Tuhaka and Warihi Campbell wish to acknowledge a debt of gratitude to all the Family Centre Staff past and present and to their colleagues in the fields of Community work, Family Therapy, Social Policy Research, Education and Training and Theology for their tireless contribution in the Journey that is Just Therapy. We particularly recognise the time, energy and commitment that each one of you gave and we have named this Journey Just Therapy in recognition of your energised search towards justice and love.

The authors also acknowledge all the Elders and Communities in which Just Therapy and The Family Centre are located.

- The Maori Community: *E te iwi, kei te mihi te ngakau ki a koutou mo nga purapura i ruia mai e koutou, kua puawai nei i tenei rai. Tena koutou, tena koutou, tena koutou katoa.*

- The Pacific Community: *Faamalo fai o le faiva. Faafetai le tauasa.*

- The Pakeha Community: *In gratitude we recognise your struggles towards a more just Aotearoa.*

Our heartfelt thanks to all our families, aiga and whanau who have to carry some of our responsibilities and commitments during our absences in our Journey that is Just Therapy. Thank you for your aroha, alofa and love.

We wish to acknowledge with gratitude all the families, aiga and whanau whose pain brought them to our door and whose determination to find Belonging, Sacredness and Liberation continue to fuel our commitment and journey.

We wish to particularly acknowledge and thank the staff at Dulwich Centre Publications and Dulwich Centre for your commitment, patience, professionalism and love that has seen us through years of Journey towards a Just Therapy.

The Just Therapy Team can be contacted c/- The Family Centre, PO Box 31-050, Lower Hutt, Wellington, New Zealand.

Chapter 1: was originally published in the special issue of the *Dulwich Centre Newsletter*, 1990 No.1, entitled 'Social justice and family therapy'. The sections at the end of this paper, entitled: 'Colonisation and its effects' and 'The Treaty of Waitangi', were written by Carmel Tapping.

Chapter 2: was originally published in G. Burford & J. Hudson (eds) 2000: *Family Group Conferencing: New directions in community centred child and family practice*. New York: Aldine de Gruyter. Republished here with permission. Copyright remains with Aldine de Gruyter.

Chapter 3: was originally published in the *Journal of Feminist Family Therapy*, 5(2), 1993. Republished here with permission. Article copies available from the Haworth Document Delivery Service: 1-800-HAWORTH. E-mail address: docdelivery@haworthpress.com

Chapter 4: was originally published in the *Dulwich Centre Journal*, 1998 No.4. This paper was created from interviews with Cheryl White, Maggie Carey and David Denborough.

Chapter 5: was originally published in *Gecko: a journal of deconstruction and narrative ideas in therapeutic practice*, 2000 No.3. The interviewer was David Denborough.

Chapter 6: was originally published in the *Dulwich Centre Newsletter*, 1994 No.1. The interviewer was Ian Law.

Chapter 7: was originally published in M. McGoldrick (ed) 1998: *Re-visioning Family Therapy: Race, culture and gender in clinical practice*. New York: Guilford Press. Republished here with permission. Copyright remains with Guilford Press.

Chapter 8: was originally published in the *Dulwich Centre Journal*, 2000 Nos.1&2.

Chapter 9: was originally published in the special issue of the *Dulwich Centre Newsletter*, 1990 No.1, entitled 'Social justice and family therapy'. This piece was written by Carmel Tapping.

Chapter 10: was originally published in the special issue of the *Dulwich Centre Newsletter*, 1990 No.1, entitled 'Social justice and family therapy'. This piece was written by Carmel Tapping.

Chapter 11: was originally published in the special issue of the *Dulwich Centre Newsletter*, 1993 No.1, entitled 'Other wisdoms, other worlds: Colonisation and family therapy'. This piece was written by Carmel Tapping.

Chapter 12: was originally published in the *International Journal of Narrative Therapy and Community Work*, 2002 No.2. This paper was created from a series of interviews with Kiwi Tamasese that took place in Wellington, New Zealand, and also in Samoa in 2000. This paper discusses some of the findings from a research project carried out by The Family Centre. The full report *Ole Taeao Afua: The New Morning – A Qualitative Investigation into Samoan Perspectives on Mental Health and Culturally Appropriate Services*, by Tamasese, K., Peteru, C. & Waldegrave, C., is available from The Family Centre.

Chapter 13: was originally published in the *International Journal of Narrative Therapy and Community Work*, 2002 No.2. This paper was created from a series of interviews with Kiwi Tamasese that took place in Wellington, New Zealand, and also in Samoa in 2000.

Chapter 14: is an extract from a paper originally published in the book *Working With the Stories of Women's Lives*. 2001 Adelaide: Dulwich Centre Publications. This paper was created from an interview with Cheryl White and David Denborough.

Chapter 15: was originally published in the special issue of the *Dulwich Centre Newsletter*, 1993 No.1, entitled 'Other wisdoms, other worlds: Colonisation and family therapy'. This piece was written by Carmel Tapping.

Chapter 16: was originally published in the *Dulwich Centre Newsletter*, 1998 No.1. This paper was created from an interview with David Denborough.

Chapter 17: was originally published in the *Dulwich Centre Newsletter*, 1998 No.1. This paper was created from an interview with David Denborough.